SELF HARM

The Essential Guide

Greta
McGough

Self-harm – The Essential Guide is also available in accessible formats for people with any degree of visual impairment. The large print edition and E-Book (with accessibility features enabled) are available from Need2Know. Please let us know if there are any special features you require and we will do our best to accommodate your needs.

First published in Great Britain in 2012 by
Need2Know
Remus House
Coltsfoot Drive
Peterborough
PE2 9BF
Telephone 01733 898103
Fax 01733 313524
www.need2knowbooks.co.uk

Contents

Introduction

Self-harm is most commonly found among young people, especially females, but is not exclusively a female activity. Females tend to favour 'cutting' – which is what we immediately think of when we think of self-harm. But modern definitions of self-harm have expanded to include a wider range of behaviours that put the body at risk. These include anorexia, burning, self-poisoning and substance (including alcohol) abuse. Some researchers demonstrate that males are statistically more likely than females to abuse substances and alcohol, or to put themselves at risk by other behaviour. (Laye-Gindhu, A.; Schonert-Reichl, Kimberly A. (2005)

This change in definition alters the statistics, so that differences between the genders are now recorded as less pronounced, simply because of differences in definition and data collection. The traditional statistic that females are four times more likely than males to self-harm is no longer as definite as it once was. In some ways the expansion of the definition is good, because it can mean that individuals whose behaviour did not meet the original definitions might now be more readily seen as needing help. Why it occurs is not as clear-cut as you might initially think. There are certain factors, and these will be dealt with in their turn, but we will also give some attention in this book to the questions that families ask, when they find that a young family member has begun to self-harm.

We will try to answer some of these questions and look at the ways forward, and at support and the likelihood – for all concerned – of surviving this unhappy time in family life.

Each of the following chapters contains an exercise or scenario, which you are asked to read and consider, before moving on. These are discussed in the final chapter of the book. You may find that your answers differ from those given in that chapter, but that is not to say one is right and one is wrong. Your answers will have grown out of your own knowledge and experience. You will be asked to consider your attitudes and preconceptions, and may find that some of these change as you read on. That is no bad thing, and the more we can keep an open mind in dealing with self-harm, the better.

There are references included here for further reading, and to help parents, health professionals and students who might want to expand their knowledge. These have been chosen because they offer clear help and guidance, and do not lose sight of the positive outcomes. It would be all too easy to read weighty psychiatric tomes, which only emphasise doom and gloom.

Any words in **bold** type will be found in the glossary. There are some words here which have slipped into common usage, but which may have a different meaning in a medical context. It is best not to assume that a word from these grey areas means exactly what you think it does.

Suicidal thoughts

Firstly, it is important to recognise that self-harm does not *necessarily* relate to suicide or even suicidal thoughts. A suicide attempt is different from self-harm, and 'cutting' has *many* other facets. Indeed, in some ways, it might provide a sort of safety valve, which allows the individual to feel pain and to suffer, but not always to progress to suicidal thoughts.

'Pain is what the patient says it is.'[

Suicidal thoughts *may* however be present, or may develop. If so, particular help and support can be offered. It is important to distinguish the underlying thinking, so that the help that is offered is appropriate to needs. There is no doubt that anyone who is self-harming is thinking of themselves in certain ways, and is emotionally vulnerable. If they are not suicidal, it would be very wrong to suggest the label to them, as it may become a self-fulfilling prophecy.

In medicine generally there is an old adage that 'pain is what the patient says it is' meaning that the degree of pain perceived is a very subjective thing. We are all different. This is equally true of emotional pain, and it is easy to look at someone else's life, and to think that they should be able to cope with their problems. To think this is to miss the point. Pain is what the sufferer perceives.

Therefore, when we listen to someone who feels like self-harming, we give them space to express their fears and feelings, and ask them to say what they think is going on. As with any issues that can be resolved by the sufferer, the starting point must always be that the individual explores what is happening and what has led them there.

There are no magic wands, but the starting point must always be in sight.

Warning signs

Anyone who is truly struggling to cope with daily life is at risk of self-harm – or at least at risk of thinking about it. The step from thinking to trying is different for all of us. It can be a slow, lengthy process or a very short step indeed.

If someone begins to describe himself as 'trapped', warning bells should ring. Anyone who describes themselves as 'useless' or their life as 'pointless' is also very much at risk. Negative thinking is already creeping into the mind. (Please note – shouting at them or demanding change is unlikely to help.)

A less recognised warning sign is indicated when someone uses the word 'duty' as a rationale for what they do. This says that they feel trapped into living in a way that is not actually their choice. The way to good mental health is to feel some sense of power and control over the events of life, and so this sense is extremely damaging in the long term.

The sense of 'duty' may extend to work as well as family commitments. It is not unknown for someone who loves their work (to the exclusion of other things in life) to become obsessed by it, and to feel guilty and anxious if they spend any time at all away from it or not achieving. In some ways this can be seen as an addiction, but it is worth remembering that for intelligent adolescents, their education *is* their work, and they may be feeling that there are extreme pressures upon them to succeed.

Family commitments which trap us, and eventually destroy any sense of self-worth and value, include trying to cope with impossible relationships. These include trying to please someone who is never going to be happy, whatever you do. Caring for a sick partner or family member can certainly take us down this route.

This is not exclusive to older people. A surprising number of adolescents are in fact currently acting as carers within the family, at a time in their life when they should be exploring and growing into their own strengths and personality.

Generalised anxiety, sometimes described as 'free-floating', is the sort of anxiety that we do not immediately say has a cause. However, this is not necessarily because the cause is unknown to us. It can be that we are simply not ready to admit to the cause, even to ourselves. If someone is in a situation of fear or abuse, the issues are so complicated that is difficult to allow space and time to even acknowledge this, let alone to examine the problem.

Risk taking is a warning sign, and is also a type of self-harm. This may include extreme sports, but without proper attention to safety procedures. Someone who has always been sporty and adventurous may move subtly into the practice of putting themselves at risk, before others really begin to notice.

Drug use and heavy use of alcohol are also ways to self-harm. While these may be recreational to begin with, when life takes a turn for the worse, there is no doubt that some of us cross a line into excessive use. Substance abuse is a highly dangerous practice, since aerosol sniffing can kill or cause *permanent* brain damage very quickly. There is no way to predict if today will be the day that this becomes true. Sniffing damages brain cells, even if it does not kill. These cannot be regained or regenerated once lost.

Certain types of obsessive-compulsive behaviour may be classified as self-harm. Obesessive-compulsive disorder is a very difficult **syndrome** to live with, and treatment is often a lengthy course of psychotherapy. This addresses the causes, coupled with behavioural work which aims to relearn patterns of behaviour. While OCD is extremely distressing, and interferes with life massively, it only really becomes self-harming when the compulsion involves features such as scrubbing with potentially toxic substances, or self-damage such as systematic hair pulling. In the latter, subjects may pull their own hair out, strand by strand. This is certainly self-harm, and the main issue is the compulsion to act. Dealing with the compulsion is the way back to health.

Finally, there is a surprising amount of peer group pressure involved in some kinds of self-harm, and adolescents in particular may find themselves part of a sub-culture where they prove that they are 'hard' – or just one of the gang – by cutting themselves. The cause – and therefore the solution – needs to be approached in another way. This will be addressed in a later chapter.

Each of these warning signs will be discussed in later chapters in much more detail. They may stem from different events in life, or even different ways of thinking. They may overlap in their characteristics. But what is important is to recognise that these are warning signs, and respond to them by making space for self-expression. Then the whys and wherefore can begin to be addressed.

Symptoms

Cutting is probably the first symptom that we think of, but there are many more ways to harm oneself than this. There are differences in the favourite ways of self-harming between men and women. Females favour taking too many tablets, and are more prone to eating disorders. Males are more physical, and have more of a tendency to excessive risk taking. This is a generalisation of course, because both genders use *all* the different approaches at times.

Other symptoms that count as self-harm, include self-burning and damaging the body by punching, banging or throwing it against something hard. Swallowing objects (such as forks, razors, etc.) or sticking things into the body may also occur.

The impulse to self-harm is usually kept a secret from friends and family, at least for a while. Many sufferers say that they feel ashamed or guilty about what they do. Eventually the activities become visible, but this may take quite some time, and a considerable amount of serious damage may have been done.

Not only suicidal thoughts

Other things which should be examined, within the context of self-harm, are items such as risk taking and eating disorders, which can also threaten life or damage the body. **Body dysmorphic disorder (BDD)** is a syndrome in which the sufferer believes themselves to be repulsive, disfigured and unlovable, however much evidence there is to the contrary. This very distressing syndrome may cause a person to starve themselves to increasingly dangerous levels, or to become suicidal, because they believe that there is no hope for them and that all is 'pointless'. It can be treated successfully, but because incorrect perceptions are in place, it can be hard for the sufferer to understand that they need help to change their thinking. At this point, families, and particularly partners, need to exercise 'tough love', which will be discussed later on.

Being a long-term carer means that life must revolve around the needs of another person. Although that person is probably deeply loved, this still means that there is a serious imbalance in life. Good mental health requires that we all

'The impulse to self-harm is usually kept a secret from friends and family.'

have *some* time and space for ourselves, and that our lives are not completely subsumed into that of another. A great deal of guilt may be involved in this scenario. Unfortunately, if a carer becomes depressed enough to begin considering self-harm, he or she may then feel that it is important that their dependent is not left to the mercies of others after they are gone. The stage is then set for a murder-suicide, or a murder-suicide attempt which may or may not completely succeed.

In some ways these are more subtle approaches to self-harm, and they do follow a different path from cutting. What is going on? Why is someone going down that route? These are questions that need answers.

That anxiety, depression and suicide are linked to self-harm is a known fact. This will be discussed later. But again, there is depression, and there is *depression*. Some sources claim that only 15-20% of people who self-harm could be categorised as mentally ill. Others put the figure higher, and certainly a much higher proportion go on to attempt suicide. Anxiety can have a crippling effect on everyday life.

'A 'cry for help' is *always* important, and should never be ignored.'

We will not refer to individuals as 'patients', here, but rather as sufferers. They may well not come into the 'patient' category. Of course they need help, guidance and support. They need the chance to talk honestly and freely about the key issues in their life.

A 'cry for help' is *always* important, and should never be ignored. From a parent's perspective, it is easy to panic, faced with a youngster who has deliberately damaged themselves. We do not want to accept the reality of the situation. Later in the book, we will look at ways forward, so that responses can be calm and sensible, and family relationships do not become increasingly strained. This only leads to increasing the distress and isolation of the self-harming person.

What individuals do *not* need is a psychiatric label, which may be unnecessary. Of course, the 15-20% can be referred to as 'patients', but it is impossible to tell, at first glance, who might fall into this category. Better to proceed carefully. Labels can be self-fulfilling, and can cause long and lasting damage to someone's life.

Exercise 1

▧ Think now of your own reasons for deciding to read this book. If there are specific questions that you would like to be discussed, write them down. Leave a space under each which can be filled in later.

▧ Now write down the reasons why you believe that people begin to self-harm.

▧ As you work through the chapters you may find information that surprises or even challenges you. Write references to each of these, and answers to your questions in the blank spaces.

Summing Up

While this book focuses on help and support for the families who care for individuals, it is also for the individuals themselves, who may want to read it and discover that their experience is far from uncommon. Their feelings are often a normal response to what has become an intolerable situation. They *can* look forward to a time when this is *not* going to be how their life is.

'There is a lot of life after self-harm.'

Health professionals will benefit from the insights that are offered here – which have been drawn from actual people. Pseudonyms have been used to protect their privacy.

There is a lot of life after self-harm. With proper help and support, and understanding of the situation, individuals can find ways to move forward, to a happier and more fulfilling life.

Many practices develop into self-harming when life becomes difficult, and perhaps changes direction. The individual's lack of a sense of control over their life is always a key issue. If this can be improved or resolved, progress can be made back towards good mental health. Each of the following chapters will help all concerned to find the ways forward to that better place.

We have a massive effect upon those around us – perhaps much more than we realise. The good side of this is that our influence need not always be negative. We also have the power to change lives for good.

Disclaimer

The results of self-harming are far-ranging, and cause considerable further serious issues within health care. (Trevillon K et al, 2011). We may not feel comfortable addressing this problem, but if we do, we will be able to help an individual back to a fuller, healthier and happier life. This book will allow us all to feel more confident about addressing the issues, professional or layperson alike. However, this book is meant as a general guide, not a replacement for professional help and counselling.

Chapter One
Definitions

History

As long as civilised human beings have recorded history, individuals have been prone to the possibility of depression and to the stresses that living in a social group sometimes bring. There are frictions in human society, and sometimes – for great lengths of time – we may find ourselves struggling to find a comfortable place in the world.

How individuals have responded to these pressures has changed over the centuries, but it is possible to see variations in almost all of the possibilities listed in this chapter, in the pathologies of previous times. In Hogarth's images of 'Gin Lane' we saw people who were so overcome by poverty and despair that their only recourse was to drink themselves into the grave. In Victorian times, middle class young ladies took to their beds with the 'vapours', ate very little and produced symptoms of paralysis. Their retreat from the world into a career of ill health is now seen as evidence of depression, and there is no doubt that those same young women would produce symptoms – although different ones – if they were alive in the twenty-first century.

In times of war, if someone becomes depressed, the opportunities to put oneself at risk are massive. Some people act without regard for self and survival, simply because they no longer care about survival.

Whenever individuals speak about the urge to self-harm, they often suggest they 'wanted the pain to prove that they could *feel* something'. Doctors describe this loss of feeling as a 'flattening of **affect**'. Affect is a medical term for emotional response. When affect is said to be flattened, the emotions are not registering normally and individuals feel cut off from the world and from everyday feelings about it. They feel that their responses are not as they should be.

'Whenever individuals speak about the urge to self-harm, they often suggest they "wanted the pain to prove that they could *feel* something".'

This is a classic symptom of depression, stress, and **PTSD.** These changes in emotional response leave the sufferer feeling that they are separate from the world and its events, and then to beliefs that they are different, usually in a negative way. Some – but not all – may begin to hallucinate, particularly hearing voices which tell them to self-harm, and constantly repeat that they are worthless.

The history of self-harm is hidden in the social and world events of particular times, each of which bring their own stressors to everyday life. Some features can be seen again and again within certain peer groups, and some are more subtle than others in their appearance.

But they have always been there.

Professional issues

Historically, discovery of a self-harm attempt has always filled human beings with horror. Perhaps this is because the potential for coming to this point is there within all of us. We feel that life should not come to this, and are appalled by deliberate self-damage and the potential waste of life.

As professionals, we may feel guilty and believe that we have failed in what we try to do.

These feelings and reactions can get in the way of acting as we should, when someone needs us to be there for them. (Grant, Biley, Walker, 2011)

Because professionals are human beings too, with their own hidden fears and anxieties, there are many reports from sufferers of being treated in a very unsympathetic manner, when they most need help. Not always, of course. But many professionals fear the idea of self-harm, and may allow their fear to overwhelm their compassion. An assumption that someone is 'attention-seeking' and therefore might be dismissed as not really in trouble is an easy answer, but in fact completely inappropriate. All cries for help are worthy of a compassionate response.

When someone appears in the emergency rooms, having self-harmed, he will be met by nurses trained in the adult branch who have not necessarily had the guidance and training needed to deal with self-harm. Paramedics also report that they have no specific training in this, and are often at a loss to know how to handle situations.

Uncertainties may translate into apparent callousness. Similarly, when someone is admitted to the mental health wing, nurses there *may* see only the 'revolving door', and be too ready to discount what has brought the patient to this point. Nurses who work in Learning Disability may find that someone in their care begins to self-harm. They may become frustrated with that person, and treat them in a less thoughtful manner.

For any health professional, the adage that we should 'walk a mile in their shoes' is often repeated, but very hard to do. During training, individual nurses are asked to learn empathy, and to always remember that there is a person who needs our help. We are also asked to reflect on our practice. Very quickly, nurses begin to cite the fact that they are too busy to give empathy the necessary time. Listening is not something that certain types of nurses see as their remit, and those that do may be conscious that there are others who need their attention.

It is important to recognise, as professionals, that we all have our failings. Every health professional should examine their own instinctive responses to self-harm honestly. It is important to look at the reasons for those responses, too. What you find there may surprise you.

'For any health professional, the adage that we should "walk a mile in their shoes" is often repeated, but very hard to do.'

- What is the actual feeling that evidence of self-harm produces in you?

- Is this more marked in certain situations or with certain (types of) individuals?

- What are the words that you habitually use, to deal with self-harm situation?

- Are these always positive and acceptable phrases?

- What are your immediate physical responses and actions?

- Does your facial and body language suggest a sense of scorn or superiority?

That we can all improve as professionals should always be recognised. Whenever someone comes to a point in their career when they believe themselves to be perfect (or even very good!) in their practice, they should recognise that a time to stop and reflect is very, very necessary.

Causes - the group

When someone self-harms, it is *usually* because they are suffering and need to express their pain. Words have failed them, or it has not been possible to find someone to talk to, safely.

Some self-harm, however, originates from identifying with a peer group in which 'cutting' has become the norm – even something fashionable. The group may regard this as a badge of honour, or a way of proving that they are 'hard'. Can it be assumed that this type of self-harm does not express mental anguish? No. To want to belong to something so badly that you are prepared to damage yourself *is* something of an extreme reaction to life. Cutting hurts.

How much it hurts has been a matter for discussion in many places. 'Sarah' explained that she knew that 'most' of her friends were cutting themselves, and became aware that there was 'a sort of competition' going on, in which people of her age experimented with cutting, in much the same way that they had experimented with soft drugs, alcohol, smoking and sex. These were all things that (it was felt) everybody should try once. 'Sarah' describes trying to cut herself, and tells us that (like her friends) she began to do this in a very small way at first, but consciously aimed to build up her tolerance to the pain.

At many other levels, self-harm is kept secret. Although a group of young people may feel that this is something that binds them together into a kind of identity, it is not shared with anyone outside that group. We will return to the power of peer group pressure in chapter 5.

What *is* sometimes described in this type of self-harm is the tendency to the development of a type of addiction. It may seem amazing that pain or self-harm can become addictive, but what appears to be certain is that those who find they need to damage themselves more and more, have a tendency to addictions in the first place. It may be that they are insecure, obsessional, sensitive, intelligent or stressed – or any combination of these. At times in life when any of these apply, we are all at risk of becoming addicted to something, because we are over-compensating for the problems that life has thrown at us.

The physiology that underpins self-harm reinforces this. When our skin is cut, we release **endorphins**, which are part of the healing process, but which also allow the brain to feel a sense of pleasure. Endorphins are also released, along with adrenaline, when we do something frightening or particularly risky. People often say that they feel 'more alive' when they put themselves at risk, by whatever means. Some also describe a sense in which the pain of the cut (or other damage) makes them feel either 'able to feel something', or that it 'outweighs the internal emotional pain'. At this point, self-harm is not a social issue, but has become a symptom of despair.

Despair

Solitary (and often lonely) individuals who begin to self-harm are expressing a sense of despair. Feelings that are very difficult to deal with and even more difficult to express have built up inside, and a way cannot readily be found to express them. Self-harm is often seen during adolescence or early adulthood, at which time all individuals are discovering who they are, and where their place might be in the wider world. If they are faced with realities that are not acceptable to them, they can suffer a great deal of internal conflict, and perhaps also **denial** and possibly **projection.**

Denial is the state where someone refuses to admit – even to themselves – that anything is wrong, no matter how compelling the evidence. The unacceptable truth may be about sexuality, the condition of the family or the loss of ideas, ideals or a belief system. This is not confined to adolescents. In later life, a situation may change so that what was once certain in life is no longer so. The collapse of a relationship, which was central to the individual's world, may be one example.

Because the world has changed from whatever provided an anchor or comfort for the individual as a child, it becomes difficult to know what to trust. This is also true if an individual *fears* the loss of a key relationship – a fear that may well be groundless.

'People often say that they feel "more alive" when they put themselves at risk.'

Therefore it is impossible to know who to turn to for help or guidance. Individuals become desperate, because they do not know where to turn for help. Self-harm can help someone to feel that they can regain some control over the world.

Self-harming individuals are sometimes heard to say, 'Well, at least there's *one* thing I can succeed at . . . '

This may seem strange, but is in fact a severe way of trying to master the terrific uncertainties that the world now presents. Inflicting pain or damage on oneself is one way of 'showing them'. (Grant et al, 2011)

'Bob' described the sense that he was 'detached from the world and from his body', which is one way of emotionally denying deeply unacceptable feelings. Here the underlying trauma was a long period of abuse. 'Bob' aimed to convince himself that it had never happened. Like many others, he managed to avoid the pain of the memory, but the result was that he felt emotionally numb. Cutting himself was the only way in which he could feel alive again.

'Jackie' described the build-up of her emotions as 'feeling as if she was going to explode'. She became afraid that her emotions would run out of control, and that she might actually harm someone else just because they got in the way. On one dark day, she found herself experimenting by turning a knife upon her own arm, and found that this drastic act 'took her somewhere else'. In some strange way the pain seemed to relieve the tension that she felt. This gave her a 'sense of relief' – a common statement among those who self-harm.

She had suffered from feelings of guilt and shame about the situation she was in, and although she had now swapped this for a sense of guilt and shame about her desire to cut herself, she felt that (because it was self-inflicted) she was at least partly in control. The terrible feelings she had now were less than the originals. She felt that she was 'taking control', by 'punishing herself before someone else did'.

The thought that punishment is a certainty which arises from guilt and confusion, is a very common one. A sense of control comes from taking charge of that possibility, and also from feeling that in some way, justice has been done.

It is important to recognise that there may be no real need to feel guilty about anything. This is often simply a fixed mental attitude that has grown out of proportion. We will return to this point later, when we look at treatment, because work that is done on returning thinking to a more realistic place is always a good first step.

Exercise 2

Now an exercise in empathy.

- Imagine a very dark time in your life, where several bad things might happen to you within a short space of time. Allow yourself to consider this, and you may find that these events may not be the worst things possible in life. It may be rather that those around you behave or respond in an unsympathetic way. If you believe that others are denigrating your feelings, or even laughing at them, you will find that the situation is much more difficult to cope with. If you find that you have a sense of being trapped in a bad situation, and cannot see who to trust or to turn to, you will find that the emotional pain increases.

- Now identify what you would like to happen, and how you would like people to respond to you. What might they say, that would make you feel less alone at this time? What would you like them to say to you?

- How would you like them to deal with you?

'Returning thinking to a more realistic place is always a good first step.'

Summing Up

- We will all experience the depths of despair at some time in our lives. If this persists, we come to the point of feeling trapped, and permanently afraid. If it seems that there is nowhere to turn, we may consider attempting to harm ourselves, but we can also find a way forward.

- The exercise in this chapter asks readers to empathise with that dark condition. However, it can also be used by someone who is already on the slippery slope. If an individual can manage to pause and imagine how he or she would like to be responded to, and what would be good if it happened, two things can be achieved.

- Firstly, the sufferer can imagine that there is the possibility of help, and a way out of despair. Because one of the features of despair is the overwhelming sense of hopelessness, being able to believe that help is possible forms a vital first step to recovery.

- Secondly, if we can identify some of the actions, feelings and responses that would make us feel better about life, it is possible to approach someone else with those responses in mind. If we know how we would like them to respond, we can ask the questions that will give us the right response.

- This is unlikely to be a perfectly successful interaction, but it can allow the sufferer to gain some sense of a significant 'other' who cares about them. Also, if the sufferer can manage to get the 'right' response from someone else, they have – at one level – begun to take control of the situation, and their self-esteem can begin to benefit.

Chapter Two

Bullying

The receiving end

Bullying is a hugely important factor in the statistics surrounding self-harm.
Probably everyone in the world has at some time been the target of a bully.
This is true, even of those who habitually bully others. While bullying is a very
sad fact of modern life, it is also possible to recognise that it can be dealt with
– either as the target, or as someone who is slipping into the habit of bullying.

Exercise 3

- Think of a time when you were the target of someone's unpleasant
  attention. This may have been at school, or it may be in the workplace or
  the family. Begin this exercise by noting where this was, how old you
  were, and what was your role within that situation.

- Now think of the person who bullied you.

- Did you recognise what they did as bullying at the time?

- What was their role (especially in relation to you)?

- What form did their unpleasantness take?

- Was it resolved, and if so, how?

- Now that life has moved on, how would you describe your bully's
  character?

- Does the memory still make you angry or anxious?

- If that person was in front of you now, what would you like to say to them?

'Bullying is a
very sad fact
of modern life.'

We will return to the possibility that *you* have made someone's life uncomfortable, later. (You may not have thought of it as bullying, but as 'toughening them up' or 'acting in their best interests' and so on.) For now it is important to examine how unpleasant the experience of being bullied can be.

Within the family, there is often one person who feels a need to control everyday life. Among children, this may take the form of petty activities such as stealing or pinching or endless nasty remarks. It is possible to observe children behaving in this way every day of the week. What is more surprising is that they get away with it.

The children who are targeted – even if they are older and bigger – seem to be resigned to the fact that this is simply what the other child does. Parents are almost always oblivious, and many never reprimand the child who is behaving badly. There are even those who consider bullying behaviour as something to be proud of.

Acceptance of unpleasant behaviour means that it continues, and always becomes worse. No boundaries are ever set which would allow either child to grow into the full person he might become. The bullying child increases his unacceptable behaviour, and grows into an adult who bullies others. (Clark, 1999) (Dellasega, 2005)

Whatever else happens for that person, he or she will never have the chance to become a fully rounded adult who enjoys successful relationships, because the habit of bullying becomes entrenched, and prevents genuine affection and closeness. His need for control will eventually lead him to be left alone and lonely.

Bullying is important in the context of self-harm for two reasons. The first is obvious – a bully can make someone's life a misery, and drive them to self-harm or worse. The second is the bully himself, who may actually find that his strategies do not always work, and that he has no habits in place that will help him to cope with being thwarted. His confusion and anger at the world may become so extreme and internalised, that he turns upon himself physically.

The power that bullies wield is always out of proportion to what they do. Bullying can cause severe psychological damage to its victims. It is easy for anyone outside the scenario to dismiss what is happening as being of no consequence, but if we do this, we collude with the bully, and cut off another avenue where people can reach out and trust. We contribute to the damage that it has done.

In the exercise we were asked to recall what it is like to be bullied. We should always make a stand against it, wherever we see it, and however slight it may seem to be. (Jennifer Thomson, 2010)

Telling

Because we tend to think of bullying as an adolescent or childhood event, we think of 'telling your parents', because we need to confide in someone with authority. However, bullying is *not* confined to our early years. Surveys conducted of workplace situations show that as many as one in three professionals state that workplace bullying has happened to them and that all too often the situation was badly handled by those in authority. (Caponecchia, Wyatt, 2011) (Dellasega, 2011)

In the workplace, a person targeted by a bully is made to *feel* like a child, uncertain of their ground, insecure and unable to achieve. The person to whom we should be able to turn is someone in a position of authority. But it is of course possible that the manager himself is the bully. In this case the victim finds himself set impossible targets, which cannot be achieved, and may be publicly mocked for failing. The more distress that is caused, the more amused and encouraged the bully becomes.

'Bullying is not confined to our early years.'

The first step in dealing with a bully is to recognise that something can be done. Most targets quickly come to feel that they have no right to complain, and no one to turn to. Self-esteem goes through the floor as a result of the cruel games that the bully plays.

Most firms, however, have a grievance procedure. This looks daunting to begin with, and a person whose self-esteem has been damaged will not initially want to become 'confrontational'. It is important, therefore, before beginning a grievance procedure to take advice from someone who understands the procedure, but who can remain impartial. A union rep can advise, or there may be someone in the human resources department who can help.

If the target is a child, the school is usually approached, but it is not unknown for teachers to see the situation as someone else's problem. This is a short-sighted attitude however, since an unchecked bully *will* develop and expand his activities, causing more and more problems as time goes by. He or she is not only damaging the progress and mental health of other children, there is every chance that he will move on to more serious activities, which will cause even more serious problems for the school (Clark 1999). The situation develops into one in which the teachers feel intimidated by a child or group of children. This is a very difficult scenario to recover from.

Children need boundaries, and they need adults to set them (Clark 1999). Managers need to recognise that they too are being manipulated by someone who simply enjoys making others unhappy, but who is destroying team morale and achievement. When we abdicate our responsibilities in boundary setting, we have abdicated our role as manager, parent or teacher.

What to do

Unfortunately, because human beings often shy away from actions that they see as confrontational, opportunities are missed to correct an unpleasant situation. When children behave badly, adults are often heard to say, 'Of course, you can't say anything, because they'll give you a mouthful.' Indeed they might. But the fear that underpins this thought – of *physical* violence – is extremely unlikely. Young people who have never learnt that there *are* boundaries in life are amazed when anyone challenges their behaviour!

To fix a young person with a stare and simply say, 'Don't do that' is certainly to invite verbal abuse. If, however, we meet that abuse without panic and with a quiet smile, the errant behaviour tends to evaporate. Most bullies have no idea what to do if people do not crumble before their demands. Verbal abuse is *also* not acceptable, and if this is in a public place (such as a shop) it should be reported to the manager. Managers should be aware that if they do not support you and insist that the person leaves, they might be seen as breaking the law. Support usually follows. If it does not, they do not deserve your business.

If the child or young person being abusive is accompanied by their parent, very often that person will say nothing at all, and will choose to pretend that nothing has happened. If, on the other hand, a parent joins in offering threats or verbal abuse, it is important to stay calm and say little. A scornful look is usually enough, and even an adult bully will stop short of physical action.

To act in this way is quite a surprise to the person objecting as well. The thought that you have stood up to a bully and stayed calm, gives a tremendous sense of achievement. When a child is behaving badly in public, nothing need even be said. Just allow him to know that his action has been seen, and that it is despised. Usually, children responded to in this way, by total strangers, actually turn away and crumble in embarrassment. Perhaps they will think twice next time.

You may think this is not a good way to behave, but in fact you could be helping a child to stay within life's boundaries, and not develop into a bully. If that is the case, there may be more than one person who is not driven to self-harm as a result.

So making sure that someone else knows what has happened is the very first step in dealing with a bully. Letting them know that their behavior is not acceptable is the second. Thirdly, we should look at ourselves, and discover if there is anything we can do to decrease repetitions.

'Bullies thrive on the misery of others.'

Reinventing

It is sometimes said that we might attract bullying, that there is something we say or do that sends a message that we can provide fun for bullies. If this becomes the case it should be no surprise that life can become so miserable that we begin to self-harm. Bullies thrive on the misery of others. The more cowed and unhappy someone becomes, the more that a bully will attack them.

We are advised to reinvent ourselves, in the face of a bully. This is not easy to do, but very possible. The first two steps outlined previously, are the beginning of reinvention. The third step is to start thinking of yourself as someone who is not afraid.

It might be possible to think first of the things you would like to say to a bully if you had the chance. Bullies are not immune to put-downs. They usually get in first. Perhaps this is rooted in the bully's own insecurity – an already present fear that they do not even admit to themselves. If this is the case, the bully who receives a confident and assertive response will not continue.

Scorn is also effective, especially the quiet variety. But it is the disappearance of apparent fear from the victim's face and demeanor that really causes the bully to pause. What has changed? The uncertainty that a change causes is very worrying to a bully, who always needs to feel in control of any situation. A change arising in another (especially the target) is enough to make them unsure of their ground.

At this point, some bullies redouble their efforts, but if they are still met with a blank calm, rather than distress, they run out of possibilities. They may always hate you, but at least it will be because you stood up to them, rather than because they have you marked as a victim.

For someone who self-harms, because life has become unbearable in this way, there is another level to the changes that can happen. 'Sally' described her experience of being bullied by a 'team' of three other girls, so that she had begun to self-harm. The damage and pain she caused herself was (in her mind) a way of hurting herself 'before they did' and that it was also a sort of punishment for being unable to cope, as well as a pain that could compete with the pain caused by the others.

'Sally' began by identifying which of the three was actually the leader, and addressed herself only to that person. She told herself that the other two were not even worthy of notice. She began to role play someone who did not care. She practised this in private again and again, so that when the bullies made their appearance, she could slip into the part she wanted to play.

Although she was nervous to the point of shaking, she managed to carry off her new image long enough to sow doubt in the leader's mind. The other two (natural followers!) were no trouble. The leader found herself unusually alone, and faltered in her attack. It was not an immediate cure for the situation, but the attacks stopped completely soon after. 'Sally', however, had acquired the habit of self-harm, and it was only later that she realised she 'did not need to do it any more'.

In effect, she had reinvented herself, and changed from someone who believed herself to be a victim, into a person with a degree of self-respect. Once she had done this, the need to cause herself pain and damage disappeared. 'Sally' began to put her energies into sport, and was soon regarded in a very different light by her classmates.

Summing Up

- Bullying is a major cause in the despair that causes individuals to harm themselves. While cutting remains the most likely response to bullying, there are many other ways to hurt oneself.

- Anybody whose actions or lifestyle put them at risk should be included in this category.

- It is possible to break the dreadful cycle that life becomes when we are the victims of a bully. It may be that the only real solution is to change the environment completely by leaving, but it is also important to change the view that we carry of ourselves. If we can practise this, when we move on to new places and situations we do not carry with us the attitudes and body language that might invite or attract a new set of bullies.

Chapter Three
Body Image and Relationships

The media

The concept of self-harm is forever tied into how we see our bodies, and there is no doubt that the media have a great deal of responsibility in this. Body ideals are promoted to the extent that some individuals believe they must be thin at all costs, even to the point of risking life. This more subtle form of self-harm develops over a length of time, but is no less damaging than cutting or risking an excess of pills, alcohol or any substance.

If someone seriously dislikes their body, it is a short step to punishing it. That this causes pain quickly becomes irrelevant. Self-harm may be fuelled by anger as well as despair, and when anger takes over, may seem to be the only way to reassert control in life.

We should not make the mistake of thinking that this is a truly conscious choice. The logic of the process is powerful and hard to escape, even though it is actually faulty. If we do not like what we see in the mirror, it can seem that the only way forward is to treat the body badly. Those who starve themselves into illness and disability are making a decision to change themselves, in the belief that this will be an improvement.

This is their way of control. But it is faulty thinking, which insists that drastic measures are called for. Once this process has established itself as a habit, body chemistry changes so radically that starving becomes essentially addictive. Addictions are hard to break, even when they take us beyond a point where life is at risk.

'Self-harm may be fuelled by anger as well as despair.'

Others look into the mirror, and see someone who (they believe) commands no respect from peers, friends or family. This individual may put themselves at risk in other ways, using chemicals, alcohol or dangerous activities. The underlying thought here is that they should prove that they are 'tough' or 'hard'.

Young men may risk their lives on motorbikes at this point, but risk-taking behaviour is by no means limited to males. Both genders may make relationship or lifestyle choices that are likely to lead to trouble, in their attempt to prove something to themselves. While it is facile to say that upbringing and background are bases for risk taking, there is no doubt that some who damage themselves as a result of excessive risk are subliminally trying to prove something to a significant (and perhaps absent) figure from their lives.

It should never be underestimated how much influence we might have on each other. It is human to want affection and approval, no matter how hard a shell we put around ourselves. Anyone who exploits that basic need is *not* a good role model, but it can be hard for an unhappy person to recognise this. An overwhelming need to belong to someone (group or individual) can colour perceptions massively.

Friends

Friends are powerful people, within our lives. In many ways we define ourselves by whatever group we believe we belong to. We all know the saying that 'you can't choose your family, but you can choose your friends' and very often if a family is felt to be less than satisfactory, friends are chosen who epitomise the opposite characteristics.

Teenage rebellion from family values is an accepted feature of modern life. There are few families who do not experience a challenge from their teenage children, and it does not mean that anyone has 'failed' as a parent. Listening to the child may help, or it may be rejected out of hand. Parents who listen *do* have more of a chance to set things right, however, and if the young person can find that they still care about the parent, the suggestion that there is another way of life may gain some leverage.

Friends may be visibly destructive and unpleasant, but they should not be condemned or banned. This will only make the child less likely to view them objectively, and the issues will become even more clouded.

It is possible to enquire after friends whose behaviour is potentially destructive. Concern might be shown as to whether they are unhappy – or jealous. Doubts can be expressed about the possibility of their goodwill.

Good friends can also be encouraged. It may be frustrating for parents to realise that good friends can never be chosen for a child. But anyone from the young person's chosen group of friends who appears to be genuinely caring, positive in outlook and encouraging rather than destructive might be welcomed.

For the person who self-harms, and for their nearest and dearest, it is important to see that there are those in our lives whose presence is damaging, rather than nourishing. It is easy to lose sight of the fact that we do *not* deserve to be punished (physically or emotionally) by those we meet every day. However, if self-harm becomes a habit, the individual is already thinking of themselves in a deeply derogatory way, and it is difficult to recognise that guilt and pain are not necessary to life.

Sometimes this has to be said. Pointing this out may be met with barriers, but if we say this to an unhappy person quietly and in an affectionate – but not exaggerated – way, the message can slowly begin to take root.

As with most aspects of thinking during self-harm, the changes are not going to happen overnight. Time and gentle support must be offered, so that a better self-image can grow.

'For the person who self-harms, and for their nearest and dearest, it is important to see that there are those in our lives whose presence is damaging, rather than nourishing.'

Exercise 4

Julie's family move to another part of the country, and Julie must leave her school. She has always been quiet, but happy and comfortable within the group of friends that she grew up with. Now she finds herself afraid of the new situation. She has no experience of establishing new friendships, and remains quiet and afraid among new classmates.

Her appetite is affected, and she begins to suffer from vomiting and headaches. Her mother notices the change in her, but feels powerless to help. Her father only really admits there is any problem when Julie is found to be cutting herself. How is her new situation affecting her body image, and what help is needed to stop this negative cycle? Which groups within the new school is Julie at risk from? How might she respond to their attention?

What might make her realise that they are a negative influence?

What can she do to escape them, into a better social environment?

In your skin

When someone is happy in themselves, we sometimes say that they are 'happy in their own skin'. This is an even more telling phrase, in the context of self-harm. If someone is unhappy enough to damage themselves, their skin (and body in general) is the first thing that they decide to attack. It is their own body that they take out their pain, anger and frustrations upon.

On the other hand, when someone becomes happier in themselves they begin to care more for their body, and even move in a newer, more confident way. Self-caring should always be encouraged, whenever the chance arises.

Summing Up

▪ A sense of friendship is essential to human beings, but not all friends are good ones whose attentions make us feel better about ourselves.

▪ Some people have a real talent for draining other's energies and making people feel bad – because of their own fears and insecurities.

▪ Because friendship is by definition usually a fairly long-term relationship, it is often difficult to identify people who are negative influences, until they have become an established feature of life.

▪ If, after a while, you find yourself saying of someone 'she makes me tired' or 'I wish for once he would see the bright side', that person is a drain on your emotional resources, and beginning to be hard work.

▪ You can point out that their negative attitudes are not doing anyone any good, but it is unlikely that this will change them.

▪ You can ask questions in the hope that this will help, but without professional training you may simply find yourself more and more tangled in their negativity.

▪ Or you can decide to cultivate someone else, to fill the role of 'friend' in your life. Friends are the most intimate part of our peer group. But peer group is much wider than friendship groups, and these will be discussed in the next chapter.

Chapter Four

Peer Group Pressure

A peer group can be defined as everyone with whom (in different ways) you have something in common. Peers include, therefore, everyone of the same age, everyone who works at the same place, goes to the same school or lives in the same area. People who relax in the same ways – for instance sport, music, drugs, alcohol or gaming – are also our peers.

Our peers include those who share our interests, and our attitudes, values and beliefs. While it is easy to believe that attitudes, values and beliefs are not something we concern ourselves with, we do have them, and they form an important core part of everyone's personality.

As with specific individual friends, peers may be positive or negative. They may energise or drain us. They may inspire, or lead us into a dark view of the world which is difficult to shake.

A major part of good mental health centres around being able to recognise that while peers are important, we do not have to share their attitudes, values and beliefs. We can consider what they represent, and distance ourselves emotionally from anything that is unacceptable.

In coping with the urge to self-harm, it is vital that good and bad peer group pressures are identified, and that we make decisions about what (and who) to include in the closest parts of our lives.

'In coping with the urge to self-harm, it is vital that good and bad peer group pressures are identified, and that we make decisions about what (and who) to include in the closest parts of our lives.'

Risk taking

What causes someone to take unnecessary risks with their health, body, and possibly their sanity? There is no doubt that excessive risk taking – which gives a 'buzz' that is pleasurable at first, has many levels. When we are afraid, and our bodies release adrenaline, the whole of the body's chemical priorities change. We get a natural chemical high, without the need for expense or illegal drugs.

This type of high is, however, just as addictive as any other chemical rush. More and greater thrills are required to maintain it, and greater risks are taken, until finally there are serious consequences.

The role of the peer group in this is crucial. There is usually a time, at the beginning, when individuals are more afraid than thrilled, but it is the pressure and encouragement of their peer group that urges them to take the initial risks. Once they have experienced the high, and addiction has begun its insidious course, they also find that they have the admiration or approval of their peers, and body chemicals are supported further by an increased sense of belonging.

An individual who was initially shy and uncertain – although possibly hiding this well – will find that peer group approval is just as addictive as the rush itself. The risks that individuals take at this point are no less self-harming than actually sitting down and cutting.

Afraid of the dark

Some of us are more at risk than others of developing in this way, and it is at this point that some personality traits are shared with those we might more readily associate with self-damage.

The individual who is basically less confident may deal with this in a number of ways. He or she may find that they attract the attention of the bullies discussed in chapter 3, or they may work hard to cover their insecurity by becoming a bully themselves. Their personal uncertainties may lead them straight to despair, and to self-harm, or they may seek the approval of a peer group or other negative relationship, which will also lead to self-harm through risk taking.

But all of these share some common ground. Each of these individuals lacks a full sense of their own self-worth, and usually suffers massive anxieties, which they hide from the rest of the world.

Sometimes as parents we may add to these fears and self-doubts by excessive expectations. Parents who 'only want the best' for their children will often confuse 'the best' with 'being the best achiever'. Few of us are destined to be superstars or Nobel prize winners, and a child who is confident and happy within their own limits is much less at risk of self-harm and has been given the greatest gift of all by his parents. The concept of 'meaningful occupation' is worth considering here. This does *not* mean occupation that brings wealth and prestige.

'Simon' did not realise that he had damaging expectations of his son. He was proud that he could cope with his son's choice of career. 'I'm okay about him being a graphic designer.' But he always qualified this by stating, 'I just want him to be the *best* graphic designer in the world.' A little bit unrealistic.

A meaningful occupation may bring no financial reward at all, but carries the reward of making us believe that we – and our lives – have some meaning. These are the activities that we define ourselves by.

Parents also often believe that they are doing the right thing by their children, by making attempts to 'toughen them up'. These efforts can take many forms, but in fact it is the child whose self-confidence is nurtured and allowed to develop, who is best equipped to deal with the world and its problems.

Another kind of parent may overprotect their child, and never truly let them develop their own coping mechanisms. Parents walk a fine line at all times, and there is no one in the world who always gets it right. When there are crises and difficulties, some parents have a tendency to blame themselves, instead of putting their energies into support and problem solving.

This is unnecessary, and may even be detrimental to the child's mental health. The best kind of parent provides guidance and boundaries as well as love for their child. This is sometimes referred to as 'tough love'. In a situation where if the child breaks the law or exceeds social boundaries, he or she understands that there are consequences, and must face them.

'We are all "afraid of the dark" in some corner of our minds, and it is here that the demons that haunt all of us at some time lurk.'

We are all 'afraid of the dark' in some corner of our minds, and it is here that the demons that haunt all of us at some time lurk. How we deal with difficult times or personal uncertainties depends very much upon the emotional habits that we have learned. But a habit is just a habit, and if it is bad, negative or counterproductive, it can always be replaced by learning good habits to put into its place.

I need to be liked

We all need to feel that we are liked. One of the bully's cruellest, most devastating and destructive tools is to make someone believe that no one likes them. This aspect of the self-harmer's personality may not be immediately obvious, but it is a fear that they share with the rest of the human race. Any support which argues against their negative self-belief will help.

Fears of being disliked, despised or simply not accepted are usually deeply entrenched, and are not going to vanish overnight, even with help. While someone whose self-image suffers in this way may be helped by counselling, there is also a school of thought that warns us that too much analysis and introspection may be counterproductive for some individuals. In these cases, a friend who simply remains cheerful and encourages happy, non-threatening activities, over a length of time, is helping the most.

We all have an 'inner child', a powerful part of our personality, who is going to influence our response to trouble or stress. If we think of the unhappy person as one whose inner child is afraid, more often than laughing, we can begin to see how to help them grow. The inner child badly needs to know that they are liked, which is different from being told that they are loved.

If the relationship that claims love is in fact demanding achievement or success, then that love is a lie. Love becomes a complex – difficult to resolve – issue in the mind, and may even be rejected as a concept completely. The inner child needs to know that they are liked – as they are. (Psychologists call this 'unconditional positive regard'.) This will provide the basis of increased self-confidence.

Accepted for the right reasons

To be accepted within a group is the other side of needing to be liked. Individuals who are unhappy in themselves will strive to be accepted, and may make the wrong, self-destructive decisions in order to find a sense of belonging. But it is also possible to consciously examine life (and perhaps its goals) and to decide what might be the right reasons for being accepted.

This involves listing characteristics that are good and universally admired, and making a conscious decision to adopt them. If these characteristics seem to be unobtainable, it is good to 'role play' them. Role play of this kind brings remarkable results, and can be increased steadily, at a rate decided by the player, until the day comes when the actions are no longer role play, but have become normal behaviour.

Will friends and family dislike the changes this brings? Possibly one or two will! But when that happens, it is time to step back and look closely at the person who does not like you becoming a better (or nicer) person. What you will see is an angry, jealous, insecure person, with huge issues of their own.

If they do not like the changes in you that are for the better, it is time to let them go. Move on to better relationships which will bring 'nourishment not punishment'.

Exercise 5

Now think about 'meaningful occupation', and what this means to you. This does not have to be paid work, but does include anything that gives you a sense of self-worth and satisfaction. It may include voluntary work, or something creative or simply active.

The positives in this sort of occupation are what make it meaningful.

What are those positives? There is no doubt that these include finding a way to describe yourself. The ability to say 'I am a dancer/swimmer/carpenter/volunteer etc.' gives a whole new impetus to self-image, as well as something new to occupy the brain and quite possibly the chance of new friends. It is important to allow time to reflect on what might work as a 'meaningful occupation' to you. When you allow yourself to discover what this would be, then you can decide upon ways forward, to begin to pursue this activity. Think about the benefits that you can expect from your choice.

Summing Up

- We must never underestimate the power of the peer group in life.

- Even those of us who avoid social interaction as much as possible, and convince themselves that they 'don't need people' are influenced by those around who may be counted as peers.

- An individual who has begun to self-harm – or who is tempted by it, either as an experiment or as an emotional statement – can never be separated from the influences of their peer groups.

- It is important therefore, to examine the individual within the wider social context of their life, and also to encourage him to do so for himself. The best – and most helpful insights – are those which can carry him forward, back towards good mental health and attitudes.

- The rest of us can only offer support. Our advice is useful, but lacks the power of an insight personally gained. The best action is just to be there, and to let the self-harmer know that you are listening.

'The best action is just to be there, and to let the self-harmer know that you are listening.'

Chapter Five
Difficult Children

School

There is a saying in psychology that 'all behaviour is communication' and this is particularly true when a young person begins to self-harm. There is no doubt that at some times in life many of us just want to be part of the world around us. Teenagers are often described as surly, younger children as difficult. When we come to adult life, we may be said to be antisocial. It is always worth trying to discover what other factors lie beneath this behaviour.

Unfortunately, children and teenagers are often labelled 'difficult' when they misbehave, and while this label may be accurate, it is in itself a block to looking any further into the issues. To say 'he's always been difficult' is to imply that this is how he is, and that there is simply no hope of any change or growth.

If someone (of any age) is behaving in a way that is troublesome or less than sociable, we should at least wonder why. Once a child has this label in school, there is every possibility that his or her reputation will continue throughout school life. Someone with this label who is anxious, worried, afraid, tired, just having a bad day or suddenly has big concerns on his mind will only be seen as their 'difficult' label, and other potential problems will never be addressed.

The teacher stands in loco parentis (in place of the parent) while children are at school, and must appear to be the adult in the relationship, if they are to succeed in their relationship with children (Clarke 1999). Many teachers fight shy of facing this part of their job, since they have 'far too much work' to take on any additional depth within their role. The mistake here is to misunderstand the phrase 'in loco parentis', which does not mean replacing parental roles and guidance. Rather, it means to be the adult in *this* situation, and to provide and maintain boundaries.

'There is a saying in psychology that "all behaviour is communication" and this is particularly true when a young person begins to self-harm.'

Writing from her own experience, Molly Clarke points out that children need clear boundaries and are in fact looking for them. What we perceive as difficult behaviour is very often children trying to push the adult, just to discover where those boundaries lie. Clarke describes how her personal decision to change her own approach surprised her class, and led to improved classroom activity, as well as greatly improved attitudes from the children.

The question of boundaries and boundary setting is central to the discussion, when we consider someone who self-harms. We were born to be social creatures, and this means that there are rules and boundaries. These can reassure us and give form to life. Or they may be uncertain and the source of confusion. Despair will follow if the boundaries of our life are unreliable, and change constantly. Other boundaries may be so restrictive that they never allow us to grow and develop. It is a fine line that we walk in our dealings with other human beings.

How does the question of boundary setting work within peer relationships? To be lonely and shy (believing yourself unlikable) is perhaps the most damaging self-image that anyone can have. It is a short step from here to feeling worthless and unlovable, and to begin to consider self-harming activities.

With others

An individual who does not perceive himself to be part of a group may quickly gain the reputation of being a 'difficult' person, and others may find it difficult to fully relax around him. While it can be difficult to say why, such a person may carry with them a vibe of uncertainty. Others are less inclined to trust him. Because this is often not consciously expressed, the attitude of his peers will also have a subtle – perhaps unconscious – effect on his own psychology and self-image. A vicious and self-perpetuating circle quickly develops.

There are many potential outfalls in this development. The 'otherness' of the less-than-comfortable individual may attract the bullies discussed earlier, or they may attract the wrong group of friends, who have issues of their own and whose priority is to cause others trouble. The lonely individual may be seen as a 'loner', without his loneliness and potential despair ever being recognised.

If we develop a negative self-image, it will colour every interaction with other people, and they will respond in kind. We know when people treat us in certain ways, and we understand without anything being said, if they have beliefs about us. The negative self-image very quickly becomes the basis of a negative and vicious circle. And although it is rapid to establish, because we are human, with human fears and insecurities, it is a hard mental habit to break.

Negative thoughts and beliefs lie at the core of self-harm. It can be difficult for anyone else to understand the self-harmer's feelings and reasons, but if this fact can be understood, we can begin to help.

Even entrenched negative mindsets *can* be altered or improved. We are always capable of changing our self-image, but it can be difficult to do this without active support from at least one other person.

Home

Parents and family have a huge responsibility in the creation of a person's self-image. Of course, families are composed of individuals who may have their own issues, or are struggling with uncertainties of their own. No one in the world is a perfect parent or partner, and if they think they are, they may well benefit from a close inspection of their own attitudes. Siblings are notoriously jealous of each other at different times, and a great deal of hidden bullying goes on within families, which can set the stage for severe insecurities in later life.

Perhaps the first thing that parents should try to be vigilant about is in fact how different children within the family actually treat each other. It is always worth pausing to observe family members. It may be a shock to discover that one of the children is actively unpleasant – either physically or verbally – to one or more of the others. Such activities are often subtle, carefully hidden from adult observation, and have long been accepted by the other children.

But observation may reveal that destructive things are happening. A child on the receiving end of 'in-house' bullying may assume that the parent knows about it, and the implication must be that they concur and do not care. Of course, nothing might be further from the truth. So if one of the children is becoming withdrawn, fretful and negative, it is the parent's job to discover what has led to this, and to set boundaries for the family that will stop the destructive behaviour.

'Negative thoughts and beliefs lie at the core of self-harm.'

Exercise 6

Think about your childhood. Do not be surprised if it was not perfect, nobody's is! But list the positives that you took away from your childhood, and disregard the negatives for the purposes of this exercise.

- Now imagine a different childhood. Imagine parents who were alcoholic, addicts, or suffered from despair and depression. Imagine that you become aware that one of your parents has begun to self-harm.

- What might be the impact of this way of life on your attitudes, values and beliefs (especially self-belief)?

- Now decide what you might need to do, to undo the psychological damage that this unhappy experience causes. Take your time over this.

Summing Up

- Children are difficult for varying lengths of time, it is an accepted fact. But to label someone as 'difficult' is not helpful, unless we take the view that this is temporary, and that we can help them to change bad or negative habits.

Chapter Six

Mental Health Issues

Problems in adolescence and early adulthood

It is in adolescence and early adulthood when self-harm, serious risk taking and the adoption of a negative lifestyle is most likely. Although the individual may be deeply unhappy, and may also feel unlovable and isolated, this is not necessarily a sign of mental illness. But these feelings should never be discounted as passing phases, because chronic unhappiness can develop into actual mental health problems very easily, if left unaddressed.

Many people suffer at least one phase of subclinical (that is, not necessarily in need of medical attention) during their teenage years. This may be purely occasional, or may recur. It may be that the lowering of mood is never fully recognised by those around.

It is during this time, when the body is changing a great deal, that hormones come into play, and cause havoc within the psyche. Pregnancy also causes huge hormonal changes, which must revert to a previous state very quickly after giving birth. The power of hormonal activity and change should never be underestimated.

Doctors and psychologists describe depression as 'reactive', in that it occurs in response to something. Years ago, we used to believe that someone might also suffer from 'endogenous' – or non-reactive – depression. This implied that a person's personality was basically depressive, and that there was little (beyond prescription medication) that could be done about it. But now the view is that something can be identified as the trigger, if we explore the issues fully. Once the triggers are identified, it is usually possible to alter lifestyle, so that the person can grow and develop.

'It is in adolescence and early adulthood when self-harm, serious risk taking and the adoption of a negative lifestyle is most likely.'

Doctors may offer medication to help someone over an acute episode of depression, but there are pitfalls. No one should be left on antidepressant medication (which is largely highly addictive) for an extended length of time. Counselling should always be made available at the same time, so that the patient can explore his or her issues, in a calmer state of mind.

Adolescence and early adulthood are also key times for the appearance of schizophrenia, which does need medical attention. But it is important to recognise that hallucinations may actually be rooted in something other than schizophrenia. Visual hallucinations may be 'flashbacks' to the experience of drug use. These are episodes that mimic or relive the trip, and which occur without any external stimulus. The person will not have taken any substance, in order to experience the flashback. Because the person's drug, substance or alcohol use may not be known to parents and family, it is easy to miss this possibility.

Auditory hallucinations, in which someone hears voices, are very distressing. They are usually unpleasant, as if someone unseen is describing the sufferer in the most derogatory terms. They may signal schizophrenia, but there is also another possibility, other than schizophrenia.

When someone is under chronic (long-term) pressure, an internal dialogue begins to rage, which is often perceived as a discussion in the mind between the voice of the sufferer, and other voices. This may be the result of bullying, extreme pressure at work or school, family expectations, and so on.

The internal dialogue itself is not an unnatural way of attempting to cope with stress. Many people do this. But as the pressures become more chronic, the voices become more insistent. They begin to interfere with everyday functioning. This is the point where internal pressure has crossed a line, and the issues that worry us have become unbearable.

If this is happening, it is important to share the fact with someone else. It is not uncommon for these harsh internal commentators to begin to suggest self-harm, ever more loudly and insistently. The only way to quieten the voices is to comply. But it is also important to realise that this may not mean the onset of schizophrenia. To treat someone (chemically) for schizophrenia who does not have it, is to cause more harm than good. All avenues should be explored by health professionals, to avoid this mistake.

A cry for help

Unfortunately, even today there are still those who dismiss self-harm or an unsuccessful suicide attempt as 'only a cry for help' or 'attention-seeking'. But to take this view is to completely miss the point. The urge to self-harm is indeed a cry for help, but there is nothing 'only' about it. If all behaviour is communication, then to cut oneself, or put the body and long-term health at risk by any means at all, is a very loud and serious form of communication. It should speak to us of the despair that the individual feels wherein he or she cannot express their feelings except by drastic and terrible means.

Anyone concerned with the topic of self-harm, either personally or professionally, should pause at this point to imagine the horror of a knife that cuts the skin. To inflict this upon oneself is extreme.

If someone is seeking our attention to this degree or is at the point where this is the only way to express desperate and overpowering feelings, the least we can do is to listen to them, and to help them to find effective professional help and support.

Therapy – talking to someone

Perhaps the one response that someone who self-harms needs is to be listened to, and to find a safe space where they can express their terrors. The listening skills that we need, in order to be useful to this individual, are discussed in chapter 8, which is aimed at health professionals, but which might also be useful to anyone involved.

Talking allows individuals to see their problems more clearly, and it is possible to speak in several different settings.

One-to-one counselling can be very beneficial. The therapist may also offer problem-solving therapy, wherein the individual explores his situation, and systematically identifies problems or issues to be tackled in an achievable way.

Cognitive behavioural therapy works very well, but should only be undertaken by someone who has the appropriate training.

'Unfortunately, even today there are still those who dismiss self-harm or an unsuccessful suicide attempt as "only a cry for help" or "attention-seeking".'

Group therapy may be available, in which individuals meet (usually once a week) to express themselves and their fears. Professional facilitators run these groups, and again more is said about this in chapter 8. Group therapy may be daunting at first, but is often highly successful.

Self-help groups are those that are run by concerned – but non-professional – volunteers, and are usually accessed via a support group. Excellent examples of successful self-help groups are Alcoholics Anonymous and Gamblers Anonymous, but there are many, many others. Sharing problems in a group *does* help, not least because it breaks the certainty that we are alone in our fears.

Therapy sessions are usually scheduled for once a week, which can be a long time for someone who is struggling against the urge to self-harm. One helpful idea is to keep a diary, so that every day feelings can be expressed, as if they were being told to someone else. This will also provide a ready summary of issues that might arise during the week, which could be discussed in the group.

'Self-harm should never be ignored as something that will lead to nothing.'

However, this diary should be private. Recording these feelings as an online blog is *not* a good idea, and may attract comments or advice from destructive personalities.

Support

It is sometimes said that if someone talks about suicide, they will not do it. This is not true. Within the urge to suicide there is a time of consideration, where the idea is explored. Self-harming incidents may well occur at this point, while the individual experiments with what can be 'handled'.

Self-harm should never be ignored as something that will lead to nothing. Statistics suggest that one in three who self-harm will do it again within a year if they do not get help. People who self harm are roughly fifty times more likely than others to kill themselves. Self harm in its traditional sense is most common among females. Males tend to favour drugs and solvent abuse, which of course is a less obvious form of self-harm.

The urge to harm oneself can be overwhelming, but it tends to come in 'waves'. It will ease after a few hours and it is possible, with support, to 'ride out' the terrible promptings. If you can learn to identify the urges before they gain full strength, it is possible to find someone or something which will help to divert the mind.

A good support group, either professionally or voluntarily run, will usually offer an emergency line for individuals to get help between meetings. If this is not the case, however, there are other possibilities.

Talking to someone – anyone – about these feelings is vital. A friend may not be available, but it is always possible to pick up the phone and talk to the Samaritans. (Many callers like to use a false name, and are asked, 'What should I call you?', so if it helps to feel anonymous, do have a name ready.) There are helplines available for other national groups too, which are very helpful if they deal with issues that have led to the urge to self-harm. Volunteers on these helplines will always be willing to listen, and to spend time while the individual talks. This can help the feelings to pass, after a while.

It is a good idea to think about coping strategies, before finding oneself overwhelmed by the urge to self-harm. 'Phil' found that water helped, and that if he could swim or take a (bitterly) cold shower, he could find distraction. Sometimes he would take ice cubes out of the freezer, and work at trying to crush them with his bare hands. These provided a harmless shock to the system, to substitute for the real pain he would feel if he cut himself.

'Becky' echoed this, and added that she began to swim as often as she could, trying to make it a part of her weekly routine. 'Ed' began to jog. Some days they felt that they did not want to exercise, but when they did, it always helped. 'Becky' recalled swimming on 'bad days' with tears streaming down her face, but which the water concealed from anyone going past.

Many others describe different sorts of exercise which they found helped, but the key to success was always to make this a part of life on the good days, so that they could more easily help when emotional problems hit.

Any exercise releases the body's natural chemicals, the endorphins. These provide a sense of pleasure, and can therefore help to lift the mood. Those sufferers who said that they had a particular kind of music that could help them often found that if they could move, use an exercise cycle or dance to that music, it was much more effective. Again, this is due to the release of endorphins.

'Gemma' found that if she did something creative, she could distract her mind from wanting to cut. She was not particularly artistic, but decided to take up sewing and embroidery. A health professional involved with her was worried by the fact that this involved the use of scissors, but in fact 'Gemma' found that it was helpful to allow her body proximity to sharp objects, and to practise using them in a new, creative and non-threatening way.

'Barney' found that drawing red lines upon his skin, in a very slow and focused way, allowed him to 'mimic' the action of cutting himself. He used a biro, *not* a sharp fountain pen. In doing this he mimed the actions of cutting, concentrating hard, but without any physical risk to himself. This brought relief.

Because the urge is very much about putting oneself at risk, this may not work immediately, and may need concentration. The troubled mind needs to convince itself that these distractions will cause pain. That they will provide a less dangerous pain – and any sense that these are foolish things to try – should be ignored

'The mind has a way of playing tricks that make us forget good things.'

Whenever we can, we should focus on positives, and record them in the diary. This is a good place to consider what sense of escape, control or relief self-harm can bring. *Then* it is possible to think of something else that can be substituted. If something new is discovered that helps the urge to pass, record it here. The mind has a way of playing tricks that make us forget good things, and if they are recorded in black and white, we can bring them back.

Part of the diary can be used to list good things about yourself. These are difficult to think of at first, but they do exist and this list can be added to over time. Every time that it is read, it can provide a quick reassurance of the positives.

It is important to minimise damage to the body, and record how we did that, although the habit may be hard to lose.

The professionals

The first of the professionals that we think of will be the GP, but there are several other people that can help. And if the problems have their roots in drug, alcohol, substance abuse or social problems such as violence or being a single parent, there are even more. Contact numbers for some of these are listed at the end of the book.

It is often difficult to approach anyone with the problem of self-harm. Parents concerned for their children or individuals for their partners often find it difficult to escape the feeling that they have failed in some way. This adds to the uncertainty about what should happen next.

If someone is found in need of medical attention as a result of self-harm (drugs, cutting, general debilitation) an ambulance must be called and the individual must attend accident and emergency, where the damage and its consequences can be properly assessed and treated. It is important to be clear and calm when calling the ambulance, without wasting time on unnecessary information about your own feelings. This will get the ambulance there quicker.

Professionals who find themselves faced with someone who has self-harmed should never be careless or derogatory about what is happening. Even today there are professionals who mistakenly believe that self-ham is less of a crisis, or perhaps less worthy of attention, than other problems.

This is not true. Someone who is putting their life at risk is making a very strong statement, and deserves to be treated very seriously. There is no one in the world who could not (given the right circumstances) be driven to self-harm, so we are particularly lacking in insight if we treat them any less seriously.

Professionals would always do well to realise that they are dealing with someone in an emotionally vulnerable state, and that whatever statements, advice or body language they offer to the patient, he or she is going to take it on board deeply and without question. This may be extended to (well-meaning) professional advice about who should be contacted, lifestyle and judgements about those who accompany the patient. The definition of a professional is someone who does not indulge in personal judgements, but who can deal with every situation as clearly as the last.

Discharge home is the norm after a visit to A and E, but the patient may be kept in hospital for a night or two. If this happens, it is unlikely that the individual is any 'worse' than another who is not. The reason is usually to do with local Trust policy.

Advice and support should be sought on return home. The GP should be informed, and it is important to ask what support he can refer to. The community mental health team are probably our most valuable asset and source of support. These can be found via the phone book, or the GP may refer. They can be particularly supportive if someone is found to be expressing thoughts about self-harm, particularly to the extent of suicidal thoughts, and will find a way to help even if the individual is not 'on the books' and known to the system.

Exercise 7

Now it is time to make two lists.

The first should be of things that give pleasure in life. This should be as detailed as possible and should include reference to people who help. In many ways, the more silly the better.

- Take care to write this list in fairly large letters, and to find somewhere that it can be displayed, and quickly read.

- The second list should include possible distractions, such as those mentioned previously, or some creative ideas of your own.

- Finally, share these lists with someone, preferably the person you are most likely to turn to in a crisis, so that they can remind you of them and suggest doing some of them when terrible thoughts overwhelm.

Need2Know

Summing Up

- It is important to focus on positives and distractions when we feel that we must cause harm to ourselves, and to do this successfully we do need to prepare for the bad times before they hit.

- Thinking about what the pain does for us, and trying to find a less dangerous substitute is central to this. But there are also things that used to give us pleasure, and it is important to remember them, and force a space back into life for them.

Chapter Seven

Families

The problems that lead to self-harm are always in one way or another a family affair. While the family may or may not contain the root cause of the urge, the psychology of the person self-harming will impact upon all members, even before it is actually discovered. His mood will already have changed, and everyone responds to that for some time before self-harm begins – and possibly a long time before it is discovered.

The impact of self-harm upon families can be massive. But it is important that responses to the discovery of self-harm do not make the situation worse, and that family members see themselves as worthy of support, too.

Tough love

The phrase 'tough love' may or may not be familiar to you. To show support we always aim to show someone that they are loved. However, it can be difficult to know how to do this. For many people the desire to show love and support is tied up in an urge to protect (possibly at all costs) and to take responsibilities upon themselves. This is rationalised as easing the burden of the troubled individual.

But this works only briefly. In fact, this approach does nothing to help the individual with the root of their problems. These will recur, because they have not been dealt with, and when they do, a precedent has been set by both parties. The relative or partner is now cast in the role of rescuer, and will find they are taking responsibility for all surrounding issues once again. Every time that this mistaken support occurs, the situation is continuing and becoming more and more entrenched.

'The impact of self-harm upon families can be massive.'

Tough love means that we show (and tell!) the individual that we love them, but that within that we make it clear that our – non-judgmental – support includes boundaries. 'You must talk to someone' is an acceptable approach. It is also possible to help the individual to arrange an appointment and even to accompany them. But to speak for them or to give your version of events is *not* acceptable.

Tough love is about helping the sufferer to gain firmer ground, by showing him where it can be, and how they can begin to move towards it. Tough love is a powerful thing, and while love is also strong, it can be strong in a negative way. Tough love, based on the needs of both parties and perhaps society in general, is better.

Parents

The discovery that your child has begun to self-harm is shocking and extremely distressing. You may well feel angry, hurt, betrayed and completely confused. The discovery of a child's self-harm will begin the rapid flow of adrenaline in your body, because the threat to a child is one of the most massive 'fight or flight' triggers imaginable.

Adrenaline works for us, in that it helps us to find extra energy to deal with an acute situation. (It may be that we must stop the bleeding and start the breathing.) But it can also produce other powerful feelings and responses, and it is important that these are understood for what they are, because some of them need to be avoided or at least curtailed.

'To become angry with someone who has self-harmed is natural, but it does no good, and may even harm the situation or damage the relationship.'

To become angry with someone who has self-harmed is natural, in that it is part of the adrenaline flow. But it does no good, and may even harm the situation or damage the relationship. The individual who has self-harmed is emotionally fragile, and already believes himself to be unlovable. Expressed anger will add to this certainty. So it is best that anger is not expressed.

It is not uncommon that our children live lives that are quite secret from us. This is not unnatural, but is simply part of the child's growth and development, in that he or she is trying to become an individual in their own right. So the discovery of self-harm may make parents feel that they have failed or are inadequate in some way. They have not failed.

58

Parents who belittle their children or push them towards extreme or unreasonable goals are damaging.

A good parent tries to respond to this situation without becoming critical or judgemental. They need to stay with the child while he or she is treated for the damage, and let them know that they are there to listen, when they are ready. Parental responses – the result of adrenaline flow – are natural, but need to be carefully handled. There is no mileage in creating more drama. Parents must always remember that they need not be alone, either. There is support available to them, and they must seek it out and allow it to work.

Spouses

The husband, wife or partner of someone who begins to self-harm will share many of the responses felt by parents, described previously. But spouses can often realise before parents that an individual's mood has become extreme, and may well have already begun to wonder what is happening for their loved one.

Spouses can also take the changes in their partner very personally, and although they will probably have asked what the trouble is, it is unlikely that they have had any answers. Someone who goes on to self-harm has already locked themselves away in a very dark place, and has become convinced that there is no one who can help. Individual reasons for this are as numerous as the individuals themselves. All too often a person who self-harms but who is also in a close relationship, will begin the secrecy by trying to protect their partner from their own fears and worries, but this quickly becomes a vicious circle when those fears are not expressed.

Like parents, spouses are subject to the adrenaline rush that causes anger and uncertainty. Partners may feel that they don't actually know this person any more – and this is particularly true if the individual has always been there for them to rely on. Again, it is important to listen, but not to become angry, critical or judgemental. It is hard to believe that a relationship can survive a self-harm incident, but important to try. Without this belief, both parties will struggle even more.

'The husband, wife or partner of someone who begins to self-harm will share many of the responses felt by parents,'

Spouses should talk to the GP about their fears and uncertainties, so that any help or support can be made available to them. Support varies in different parts of the country, but there is always something or someone who can offer it

Children

The children of someone who begins to self-harm have a particular set of problems to deal with, and we should never forget that they probably need help and guidance in their own right. Children look to us as parents to be strong and capable. They may not always agree with us but they do need us to fill that role. Someone who has begun to self-harm is no longer a strong, capable person, and children will know this, however well hidden.

Children learn behaviour from the adults around them, and deal with the world by whatever coping mechanisms they see adults use. They are not to know that a response to the world is faulty and dangerous. There are of course many occasions when self-harm becomes successful (or nearly successful) suicide attempts, and the child is the one to discover the body. This is traumatic for anyone, but particularly a child, who will have a long hard struggle ahead of himself, trying to make sense of what has happened.

As in messy divorces, children (especially the youngest) tend to believe that the adults' problems are something that they have caused. It may not be immediately obvious that the child is thinking this, and after a length of time this idea can be difficult to dislodge.

'Janet' says, 'I was an inconstant mother' and lists the emotional neglect, hostility, unpredictability and confusions that she brought into the lives of her children. A turning point for her was when she realised that they were learning behaviour from her.

All of these issues need particular attention for the child. He or she may well need professional help and guidance to grow through this difficult time, and this should always be someone who specialises in dealing with children. Play therapy, writing and artwork are successfully used to help children, and the skill of the adult professional is never to put their own (or indeed any adult) interpretation on what is being said, done or created. The child must explain what he does, in his own words and his own time. As with any counselling situation, it will take time for the child to trust the therapist and the situation, which can never be rushed.

Friends

We return to the role of friends several times within this book, but here it is important to mention the impact of self-harm upon the friends of the self-harmer. The most common reaction is guilt, when we discover that someone we thought we knew well has begun to self-harm. It is easy to think that (as a friend) we should have been able to see the warning signs.

However, the likelihood is that before self-harm has become a reality, the individual has long since begun to distance himself from anyone who has been close. We should not feel guilty, since there is a limit to what we can do to help someone who is busy establishing barriers and distance. There are no official counselling routes to support the friend of someone who has self-harmed. But it can be a traumatic experience and they may benefit from some time spent on the phone to the Samaritans.

Professional help

How professional help works is detailed elsewhere, but the important thing to know is that it does exist, not just for the self-harmer but also for all concerned with them. Different help suits different needs and situations, and it is important to accept the right kind of guidance and support.

Not every GP is familiar with everything that can be offered, although most do have a range of possibilities to offer. The community mental health team will certainly know whatever is available in the local area, and will also know of support that relates to specific problems, such as drugs, alcohol, gambling and domestic violence. It is important to ask about these.

'The most common reaction is guilt, when we discover that someone we thought we knew well has begun to self-harm. It is easy to think that we should have been able to see the warning signs'.

Exercise 8

What should we do if someone we know begins to self-harm? Could you direct someone to more information or a self-help group? Could you reassure them that they are being listened to?

- Make a list of the things that you think it is most important to do. Now make another list of things you should not do (or say). Discuss your responses with someone else, and decide how you would like someone to treat you, if you needed help.

- Within your list, add in actual phrases that might help.

'. . . decide how you would like someone to treat you.'

Summing Up

- Whatever our relationship to the person who self-harms, we will always feel the event as an emotional point in our lives.

- We can learn a lot about ourselves at times like these, and it is important that the lessons we carry forward can become positive ones.

- We may know that we are not to blame, but it can be difficult not to feel guilty. If there *was* something (for instance, bullying or abuse within the family) which we wondered about but were never brave enough to deal with, our guilt may be justified. But it is still important to look at this honestly, and to resolve to be a better friend, a braver advocate and more genuinely supportive within the situation, in future.

- There is no doubt that we can, while adrenaline takes over our emotions, easily say or do the wrong thing in an already fragile situation.

- Silence is better than angry words. A simple hug will go a long way, or a hand held – without words – just to let the sufferer know that you are there.

Chapter Eight

The Professional Point of View

While this chapter is aimed at the health professionals themselves, it is not exclusive. There are many among us who are involved in the help and support of those who self-harm, but who are not health professionals. These include all those who are involved in voluntary work, support groups, Samaritans and so on. Concerned family and friends also use their listening skills when offering support and it is important to be clear just what those skills are.

Listening

What makes a good listener? There are several key factors. We know that someone is listening to us genuinely and attentively if they pay attention to us, and maintain (non-threatening, non-staring) eye contact. There are many people who believe that they do this well, but who in fact fall short of best practice.

Body language will almost always betray us if our minds are not fully focused. If someone is thinking ahead to the next question, the person being listened to will 'sense' that very quickly. In fact they are picking up on the subtle clues sent by the listener's body language. The only possible response to this is not to trust the listener, and to increasing set distance from them.

The only cure for this is to actually listen fully and with full attention. The listener's questions are not important. What the speaker wishes to communicate will emerge – and all the better without pushing or prompting, because it is the speaker who sets the pace. This means that the speaker can relax, and learn to trust the listener. Key issues will never be shared with a listener who has not gained that trust.

Good listeners speak as little as possible, without being actually silent, which would be intimidating. Often it is enough to murmur or to make a small noise of assent, which lets the speaker know that he or she has been responded to, but which does not break their flow. It is alright to be silent, and while many people dislike silence, the speaker can learn that silence can also be a comfortable part of communication, and allow themselves to relax.

'When someone is listened to by a good listener, the insights that are achieved also bring a sense of achievement, a feeling which has been badly lacking in life for those who self-harm'.

Reflection is the skill of echoing what the speaker has said, perhaps as a question. 'Mirroring' is the term given to the body language that echoes the speaker's body language and posture. Both of these help to reassure the speaker that he or she is being listened to, and that he is not being threatened or discounted in any way. Echoing by reflection or mirroring tells the speaker that nothing he says is being judged or commented upon.

Good listeners never offer their opinions on what is being said. If an opinion is asked, the response should always be to say that it is the speaker's opinion and feelings that matter. The speaker can then be encouraged to explore those feelings further, and an even better exploration and insight can result.

Being listened to and being able to find a safe space in which to express feelings is crucial to regaining health. When someone is listened to by a good listener, the insights that are achieved also bring a sense of achievement, a feeling which has been badly lacking in life for those who self-harm.

Being a good listener is therefore much more than acquiring a skill. You may also be saving a life.

Facilitating a group

Group work may be offered in several situations. This is particularly true if the patient finds himself offered some time at a psychiatric day hospital. Group work includes several other people who may or may not share the same problems. It should always be remembered that if one-to-one counselling can be scary enough, and will always take time to relax into, the presence of others, probably strangers, must be even more so.

Some groups are 'closed', which means that they run for a set number of weeks, and aim to address a particular type of issue. They have a start date and must run their course without anyone new being added to the membership. There are obvious problems with this approach. If a date is set for a group to start, and it runs for six weeks, then someone who presents with similar problems after it has started cannot join and gain the benefit for quite some time. They must wait, and will have to cope without the support that group might have offered. They may well (subliminally) feel further marginalised or discounted.

Many other groups are 'open'. They do not have fixed start and stop dates, and membership is fluid. People can be invited to join, and attend, only asked to introduce themselves at first and to listen.

Best practice in group work, which is known as facilitation, is for *two* professional leaders to work with the group. They should not sit next to each other, which would always suggest an 'us and them' situation. This prevents a professional from dominating the flow of the group, and allows the focus of the group to range around the room, avoiding the sense that it is in any way a lecture or a lesson.

Tensions develop sometimes within the group, and each of the facilitators should always be aware of these. Both facilitators have equal status, and either can say, 'Hang on, let John finish' or, 'Is that what you were describing the other week, Julie?' so as to keep the balance of the conversation flowing.

The facilitators must practise keeping their body language open, non-judgemental and genuinely friendly. Timing is important within group work, just as in one-to-one work. All concerned should know when the session is going to end, and a group that lasts more than an hour is unlikely to prove beneficial.

Groups should start promptly, and members should be encouraged to be on time. If someone makes a habit of being late, they are trying to draw attention to themselves in some way – perhaps which cannot comfortably be discussed in the group. One-to-one time should always be made for them to discuss this.

About ten minutes before the end of the session, one of the facilitators (preferably not the same one each week) should mention the time, and that the session is coming to a close. Particular contributions may be mentioned and it is important to say 'thank you' and 'well done' to anyone who has spoken in a significant way, and to the group in general. Sometimes a gentle, achievable target may be set for the next week. All members should leave with a sense of achievement, or the knowledge that they can speak privately if there is something troubling them.

Finally, any health professional should ask herself regularly –

- What do I understand by listening skills?

- What do I understand by open questions?

- If I believe I can only spare this person limited time, what is the best way to handle the situation, so that the sufferer becomes calmer?

- Can I find a calm stillness within myself, which I can call upon so that I act gently and professionally in a difficult situation?

- Can I document what is happening here without any language that includes evidence of bias or prejudice? (Remember, what you write in the records is a legal document.)

- Is anyone around likely to interfere with my efforts to calm the situation, and if so can they be delegated to deal with some other aspect of the situation?

- Will we debrief (and record) after the event?

- What can we all learn from how we operated? Imagine yourself to be the team leader, and consider what guidance you would give to someone less experienced than yourself to help them, and in what way you would use your words, body language and tone of voice?

- Can you use this so that everyone (patient, relatives and professional team alike) learn from the experience?

Exercise 9

If you are a health professional, think now about the people in your personal caseload. Some of them have things in common, and once you identify these, you have the potential for a group. If you are part of a voluntary support network, you already have your group. But there are certain questions to be asked before you begin:

- What is the focus of this group?

- Is it general or specific?

- Who can you rely upon to co-facilitate with you?

- What protocols might you want to put in place?

- Is this to be a single-sex or a mixed group?

- Is this a closed group, or will people be able to join at any point?

- And what is the optimum number of members, excluding yourself and your co-facilitator? What sort of record will be kept?

- How will you explain the group to potential members, and what might you say to persuade them to join?

- Answering these questions before you begin means that structure is in place, any issues can be resolved, and the group will not flounder within a few weeks. What are the rules and boundaries?

Summing Up

- These approaches to helping those who self-harm are universal, and provide the basis of good practice in any situation.

- While the individual will find himself listened to; and regarded, he will learn that he is not under pressure to perform in any way. Progress can be made at his own pace.

- The individuality of the individual is key.

- There is a very true saying in health practice that 'pain is what the patient says it is'. While we think of this in terms of physical pain, it is no less true of emotional pain. It hurts when the patient says it does, and he is the one to judge when it gets better.

Chapter Nine

Self-Esteem

Anyone who self-harms has lost the majority of their self-esteem. If the self-harm comes in the form of excessive risk taking, the individual may present as someone who is devil-may-care and enjoys a degree of confidence and bravado. This can be a carefully crafted front, disguising a very insecure personality.

Such individuals are particularly difficult to help, since they take a great deal of pride in the image that they project to the world. There is no doubt however that excessive risk taking, like anything else that potentially threatens human life, is a form of self-harm and in many ways a (well-hidden) cry for help.

Human self-esteem is a very fragile thing, and may be a construct that is built upon the flimsiest of foundations. Good mental health depends upon good self-esteem, and it is vital that the growth of good self-esteem is addressed.

'Human self-esteem is a very fragile thing.'

Needs and wants

Needs and wants are very different from each other, and it is important to look at those differences now, so that we can see what sort of part they play in our metal health.

Something that we want may feel pretty compelling. There is no doubt that wants can become the focus of our life, so that all our thoughts and energies are taken up with trying to gain them. If we have no hope of gaining what we want, we may waste an incredible amount of time – years even – daydreaming about the possibility. This can come to the point of obsession. Obviously to be this preoccupied with something we want is far from healthy, and there may come a time when we have to face the fact that we need to step back from this obsession. We *must* stop defining ourselves in an unrealistic way.

Something that we need is a lot more basic. A want can feel like a need, when we let it get out of hand, but it is not really. The real main difference between these two is that a want can be counterproductive in our mental health, causing us to have a very skewed view of the world and our place within it. A need (as defined by Abraham Maslow, 1943) is something that can support us in our mental health, and should always be worked towards.

We will discuss Maslow's Hierarchy of Needs in a moment. But first on Maslow's list of needs are the physiological needs, closely followed by safety needs.

Physiological needs include air, water, food and sleep. Without these, mental health is impossible, and we must always address these first. Safety is also a basic. If we feel unsafe, mental health is going to suffer. This is the true definition of a need – not just something we want very, very badly.

It is important to look at wants and their relationship to needs (as defined by Maslow) here, because this is where we define ourselves, and where we can lose sight of the self-esteem so necessary to mental health. It is also here that we can see possible things to focus on, to bring us back to mental health. Maslow's Hierarchy of Needs is more than just a description. It can also be a very useful tool, helping to guide individuals away from self-dislike and towards acceptance of self, and a happier, fuller life.

Maslow's Hierarchy of Needs

Maslow's Hierarchy of Needs is usually represented as a triangle. This image is used so that we can readily see the absolute essentials of life at the base, supporting those that follow.

To maintain (or return to) mental health, we must first make sure that the very basic physical and safety needs are in place. Maslow famously wrote that he studied healthy human beings to arrive at his model, because 'the study of crippled, stunted, immature and unhealthy specimens can yield only a cripple psychology and a cripple philosophy'. His aim was to help people to return to mental health, rather than just to label them negatively. He included such figures as Albert Einstein and Eleanor Roosevelt in his study, as well as a group of very high-scoring students. It could be argued that these – often larger than life – individuals were not representative of the world in general, but in fact studying them allowed Maslow to describe how we all might achieve, in terms of good mental health.

Several other writers have argued that basic needs cannot be structured into a hierarchy. However, Maslow's is a good model, when we look at those amongst who need to regain their sense of self, and try to help them find their way back to self and purpose in life.

Physical needs

Maslow lists the following as essential, basic physical needs:

- Breathing – Air could be included here, and it should be recognised that pollutants are toxic in the right amount, and will cause disorientation and confusion. By extension, breathing substances such as glue (for recreation) or toxic fumes (through not taking safety precautions in some kinds of work) will cause severe problems that are sometimes very difficult to remove.

- Food – Reasonable nutrition, rather than just quantity. A hungry person cannot focus on improving his mental health. That need has to be met first. But poor diet can affect us much more deeply than by simply causing hunger. The argument runs that a person's mental health cannot be successfully improved, if he or she remains hungry. The body has too much to struggle for before it can allow energy to be expended upon regaining mental health. This argument can extend to bad nutrition, such as too much caffeine, junk food and so on, all of which can adversely affect the mental state, if taken in large amounts.

- **Homeostasis,** or 'steady state' – Human beings are physical creatures who need to live fairly balanced lives, within certain limits or parameters. If an individual is forced to live in an 'extreme' situation, both physical and mental health will suffer. This item overlaps with the safety needs described in the next level. Fear, threat, bullying and the stress of constant uncertainty are part of both homeostatic and safety needs. We have already looked at the impact of these on people who decide to self-harm, in earlier chapters. Again, it is important to regain a 'steady state', if an individual wishes to regain or improve the mental health.

- Sex – This is listed as a basic need, but its position in the hierarchy is ambivalent, since it is also included in other levels of the triangle. Love and belonging is the most notable of these. But sex can be included in all levels of the hierarchy, to a greater or lesser degree. How much of a need sex is at different levels is a very individual thing, but should never be underestimated.

- Sleep - Anyone who is deprived of sleep will suffer physically. Their mental health will deteriorate. If sleep is disturbed so as to prevent a person from dreaming properly, they will begin to inhabit a strange, twilight world which increasingly loses touch with reality. **Paranoia** quickly develops. In many situations, sleeplessness is a symptom of something else, for instance depression. The fact that sleeplessness causes a person to feel worse, both physically and mentally, can be the start of a very serious vicious circle.

Safety needs

'Why might individuals choose to put themselves at risk? This is a key question, in the context of self-harm.'

Once basic physical needs are met, the next most important needs are those of safety. Some of Maslow's critics would argue that safety needs are just as basic as physiological needs, and there is no doubt that in terms of mental health and wellbeing, they are *very* close. So you may choose to regard them as just as basic and essential as physical needs. This is where – for many people – a need for a fairly ordered life, and the sense that they are in control of what happens to them, comes strongly into play.

There are of course many people who enjoy a sense of risk in life, and for whom a well-ordered life would be an unpleasant thought. Risk taking can, however, become addictive, and even if it does not, it can lead individuals into some very dangerous places. This is where both mental and physical health might be put at risk by trying increasingly dangerous practices. Substance use is again a case in point.

Why might individuals choose to put themselves at risk? This is a key question, in the context of self-harm. As we have seen, for some who choose to self-harm there is an increasing wish to approach a real danger point. The psychology behind this may be rooted (for some) in a need to punish oneself. Or it may be a growing addiction to both pain and danger. While a person may see these thrills as part of what gives life meaning, they may also risk losing life, eventually.

Personal safety

Personal safety is the first thing to consider at this point in Maslow's list. How far is the individual's life at risk? What is causing that risk? Are other people a threat or an incentive? One thing is sure, a life lived in a 'risk' situation is unlikely to gain improved mental health.

Financial security

Financial security is something most of us strive for and many of us dream about. Different individuals believe in different ways to financial security. While a career is one way for some, others dream of sudden fame and fortune, lottery wins, and others still believe that it can be achieved by crime. Whatever the course adopted, there is no doubt that most people in our society are forever struggling towards something more, in terms of finances.

The few who are genuinely unconcerned by finances live on the edge of society, but manage to be very happy, because money worries do not overwhelm them. It is hard to live in our world without worrying about money, but it is important to recognise that those worries can be greatly over-exercised. Another obsession, with money this time, could get in the way of good mental health.

The real point about financial security is that a person believes they are secure. If they cannot believe this, there is no amount of money in the world that can make them feel safe. Once again, the answer lies within self-perception, and learning to feel okay inside.

Health and wellbeing

Physical health matters. If someone is suffering from a long-term illness, they will eventually begin to feel trapped by it, and may come to resent the loss of the life they once knew. As we age, people often feel angry about the loss of abilities that they have always previously taken for granted. As I once heard someone say to a doctor who was prescribing antidepressants rather than looking at physical symptoms, 'If you felt as ill as I do, you'd feel depressed too.'

In health care these days we tend towards the **holistic** view of people, and try to see them as whole people who are a combination of physical as well as emotional, social and spiritual attributes. These will be discussed further in chapter 10, but for now it is important to see that a sense of good health must be included in the safety needs.

Individuals who appear to suffer constant ill health, and who worry about all sorts of serious illnesses, have moved into a serious, unhealthy preoccupation which again can prove a vicious circle in terms of mental health.

Love and belonging

'Individuals suffering from the belief that they are not loved, and that they can never fit into everyday life are blocked from achieving good mental health.'

Individuals suffering from the belief that they are not loved, and that they can never fit into everyday life are blocked from achieving good mental health. This is the third level in Maslow's Hierarchy of Needs. Again, this is particularly significant when we consider people who self-harm. We have already said in an earlier chapter that one of the key factors for individuals is that they appear to have no close friend. From the parents' point of view, the physical and safety needs may have always been met. But sometimes – especially during adolescence – young people lose a sense of their own self-worth, and believe themselves to be unlovable outsiders.

The reasons for this are multiple, and are discussed elsewhere in this book. In the context of Maslow's model, it is important to recognise that this need must be addressed, so that the individual can move on, back towards mental health.

Esteem

If the need to feel loved and lovable is addressed, it is possible to move to the next level of need. This is the need for esteem – both self-esteem and the esteem of others. There is no doubt that the sense of love and belonging, which was lacking in the previous stage, is a question of perception. The individual may well be loved, and may well have the respect, esteem and admiration of others. What he lacked in that previous stage was the perception that this was so.

To achieve his esteem needs, he must allow himself to believe that he has love and a group of people to belong to. Then he must move towards allowing himself to improve his self-esteem. Some exercises that can help with this are discussed later.

The signs that a person lacks self-esteem are evident when he is listened to, and listening is a great tool for allowing him to grow and express himself. In this way he can begin to develop the necessary self-esteem, by discovering more about himself, and by giving himself credit for his good points. Self-esteem and the esteem of others is a vital point in the route to gaining full mental health.

Self-actualisation

At the top of Maslow's triangle is a strange heading – Self-actualisation. What on earth does this mean? The individuals that Maslow studied were all successful, energetic people, who seized life and rose to its challenges. By living in this way, they could be said to epitomise good mental health. They lived full lives, contributed to their part of society and appeared to enjoy what they did. They probably suffered from dark days, like everyone else, but this did not stop them from moving on and back into the full flow of life. Self-actualisation can therefore be said to be what we might all aspire to, in terms of good mental health.

But it is important to remember that probably more than half of these people were regarded as eccentric. Does that mean they were mentally unwell? Not at all. Their eccentricities were in fact the *creative* side of their natures, which they allowed to blossom.

Sadly, in certain circumstances, the actions and energies of any of these people could have been construed and labeled negatively. Many very clever, creative and highly talented people have slipped over into depression and bipolar disorders. But creativity per se is also the best possible way of expression, listening to self, and learning to grow. It is also a key factor in self-esteem. *Any* creative act – however badly executed – helps to raise the mood, so someone who allows themselves the opportunity to create, dance, exercise or help the world in some way is doing themselves a lot of good.

Exercise 10

Carrie has been lacking in energy for a while, and has lost interest in her friends and the things she used to enjoy. She no longer feels that she is loved – or even deserves to be loved, and has started to think that the world would be better without her.

She has cut her arms several times, but no one knows. She wears long sleeves and hides the evidence. At first she was shocked by the pain, but now feels she can cope with it better, and is beginning to cut deeper. She began to feel that she was very distant from the world, and that her feelings about it were no longer real. It seemed to her that she was cut off from everything by a 'blanket of cotton wool', where she felt no real pain. She wondered if she would ever feel things properly again. Because of this, she began to pinch and scratch herself, and then to experiment with scissors to see if she could produce a response in herself.

She is found bleeding from a serious cut, and an ambulance is called. What might follow? Who might ask her questions? How might she respond? Will she talk? Will someone listen? Now she has cut herself several times, but no-one knows. . .

What might her parents feel, and how might they react?

What would be a good, positive thing to draw her attention to, about herself?

Summing Up

- Within this chapter we have looked at the needs that are essential to the development of good mental health – or a return to good health, if a person is struggling. We recognise that there are ways forward, but in times of trouble it can be difficult to see what those ways are.

- Maslow's hierarchy is shown here as the model, because it demonstrates, step by step, the needs that must be met, before we can grow emotionally.

- The image of the self-actualised individual is one that we should hold on to. That happy, creative, energetic person could be any one of us. What we need to learn is how to accept certain good things about ourselves. This allows us to move up through Maslow's triangle, back towards full mental health, each step building securely upon the last.

Chapter Ten

Good Health and its Promotion

What keeps us well?

How do we define being 'well'? Although ill health may be evident, good health can mean different things to different people. Individuals who are overweight, smokers who struggle with breathing or are anaemic may look unwell to the rest of the world, but may insist that, 'I have my health, so I don't need to change anything.' When we begin to look at health in general, we quickly become aware that mental and physical health are closely intertwined.

Attitudes that are potentially unhealthy can impact upon the physical, and vice-versa. The question 'what keeps us well?' is therefore much more difficult to answer than we might at first imagine. There are some guidelines, however, which most people would agree upon, unless we ask them to apply these to themselves.

Health is more than the absence of disease. Among the things that keep us healthy are good diet, exercise, fresh air and attention to any problems that arise.

Diet is about healthy eating – not diet regimes and a good diet is one that includes fruit, vegetables, meat or other protein and keeps fats, sugars, high-carb snacks, alcohol and fry-ups to a minimum. We are conditioned in our society to eat junk from an early age, when food that offers no nutritional value is constantly offered as comfort or reward. The habit of bad eating is difficult to break, but as 'Shona' remarked – 'There is no food or drink that I want more than I want to be healthy again.'

'Health is more than the absence of disease.'

Exercise is also a daunting prospect for many of us. The trick is to try something, even if only for five minutes a day, building up times over an extended period. The key is that it should be a regular part of daily routine, rather than an occasional 'blast'.

Fresh air may be difficult in the middle of a city, but walking or visiting the park is still better than never going out, or always driving. Every day, even if conditions are not ideal, we should walk at least a hundred yards. The aim is always to increase this but again, if it can become routine and regular, this small achievable amount will work wonders.

Finally, attention to any problems that arise is essential. Many people ignore problems, because they believe they know what the doctor will say if they approach him. But they could be wrong, and getting his opinion may save a life.

We do know what the bad things are within our diet and lifestyle. The impetus to change these habits must always come from the individual themselves, but it is easy to claim 'I can't do that; I've no willpower' and never actually begin to make the small changes that are needed. We harm ourselves – and shorten our lives – by failing to make necessary changes.

How we treat the physical body impacts massively upon state of mind. Good – or improved – physical health will lead to improved mental health, and should always be attempted, when we want to move away from self-destructive mental habits.

More about exercise

We are all aware that a little exercise is good for the body. Joints keep working longer, weight remains at a healthier level, organs and systems work better for longer. But the impact upon mental health is also a facet of physical activity. Whenever we exercise, a number of things happen.

Breathing increases in order to carry more oxygen to the brain and the muscles. This means that each of these areas is benefitting every time we exercise. If exercise is difficult, activities such as gentle yoga focus upon breathing patterns, and may also help.

Adrenaline is released by the body, which allows more activity to take place. This can be the beginning of a positive cycle, benefitting much more than just the muscles and systems that the exercise involves. Adrenaline has a positive beneficial effect upon attitudes, feelings and self-image. While these benefits are brief, once they have been experienced, the individual will know that he or she can experience them again, and begin to enjoy those new and re-remembered aspects of himself.

Endorphins are released when we exercise. These are sometimes described as the body's 'pleasure' chemicals. They occur naturally as a result of exercise, and although we may feel the discomfort of aching muscles at first, we should also allow ourselves to be aware of the pleasant tiredness that comes from having exercised. To focus upon this pleasure is to allow the brain to begin establishing new – positive – mental habits, which we will pursue in the future by repeating the exercise.

When we despair of life and need to completely revise our self-image, it is difficult to know where to start. Exercise allows the body's natural chemical responses to give us that beginning. There is no one to compete against, except ourselves, and every few days we should aim to increase what we do. Routine is essential however gentle our exercise, and even if we never increase our activities.

How to promote good mental health

The promotion of good mental health can be equally tricky. Certainly if the endorphins described above can be brought into play, we will begin to feel better about ourselves. But there are other ways forward, too. It is important to approach the problem from all possible angles.

Anyone who has begun to self-harm, for whatever reason, is in the grip of negative mental attitudes and beliefs. This is true even when there appears to be no real underlying pathology, but peer group pressure is actually the main factor. 'Cutting' in particular requires a certain commitment to the negative. Using destructive drugs and substances may begin as a social act, but quickly lead to negative emotional changes.

'Adrenaline has a positive beneficial effect upon attitudes, feelings and self-image.'

When we work together in group a good place to begin is with the question 'who are you?' and the answers will always be revealing. In the 'black hole', people can only describe themselves in terms of their relationship to others, and self-description is difficult because of the negative sense of self. Someone who is struggling emotionally may even not be able to answer this question, and may find themselves in tears. This does not mean that the question should not be faced. Any self-description should be gently encouraged and smiled upon. Then it is important to refine the question.

The next question may be 'who/what would you *like* to be?' or 'who were you (describe yourself) five/ten years ago/when you were at school/the last time you were happy? What did you want to be in those days? What were you good at? What were your dreams and beliefs?'

'The goal of all therapy is to help the sufferer to move on, away from the problems, fears and circles that keep them emotionally trapped'.

From the answers to these questions, it is possible to discuss the way forward. Many people find that only certain aspects of their life and personality are encouraged during their formative years. Parents believe that they are acting in the child's best interests, but in fact they can be doing untold damage. Rewards and approbation may be always tempered with derogatory asides. Activities that bring pleasure or emotional release may be discouraged. The urge to creativity may not be understood.

That we all have a creative side is often not recognised. We do not have to be good at anything.

Moving on

The goal of all therapy is to help the sufferer to move on, away from the problems, fears and circles that keep them emotionally trapped. All concerned must continue to believe that this can be achieved, even though it looks daunting – and perhaps impossible – at first.

It is also important that goals and timescales are not set for the self-harmer. Recovery must be at the pace that they feel they can move, and always in small, achievable milestones. For someone else to impose their idea of recovery on a sufferer would do much more harm than good. This may be frustrating for the would-be carer, but moving on is not about the friend's/parent's/professional's ego, and we should stay away from the situation if we cannot hold back when necessary.

Exercise 11

Ellen was a success in terms of the world. She was a maths teacher, and had been promoted to the post of Deputy Head. When she came to the group, she appeared to be a very stern, organised lady who had her life under control, and who guarded her privacy fiercely.

Yet Ellen was self-harming. She had struggled against suicidal thoughts for a long time, and had become more and more isolated. She said that she hated the school, she hated the kids, she hated her colleagues and above all, she hated herself. The question 'who/what did you want to be when you were fourteen?' made her very angry. Behind the anger lay the fact that as a teenager, she had been found to be good at academic work, especially maths. Her successes in this were always praised and rewarded. 'But what did you want to be?' we asked her, and she found herself telling the group – 'A belly dancer.'

But any impulse towards creativity had been discounted as unimportant when she was young, and often actively discouraged. There were some smiles in the group at the thought of this middle-aged lady learning to belly dance, but of course, many ladies of all ages do this.

After some weeks, working with professionals one-to-one and within the group, Ellen found that she could see enough of her original self to understand that to become a fully-rounded person, she needed creative activity in her life, as well as work and more work. She never did take up belly dancing, but began to experiment with ceramics, and produced marvellous, brightly coloured pots.

This regaining the balance in her life, and keeping a space for the creative, led to her full recovery.

Fortunately, moving on can quickly form the basis of a positive cycle of mental health. Even the smallest achievement – which should never be disparaged – can be praised and emphasised, in order to lay the renewed foundations of self-esteem.

Individuals should be encouraged to keep a diary, so that they can easily remind themselves of the progress that they have made. There are bad days, of course. The self-harm situation is not linear. A good support person will always be able to remind them that bad days happen. But on the whole, the proportion of good days is increasing. If this can be accompanied by gentleness, kindness and possibly even physical contact, all the better.

Moving on is what we aim to do, and any form of progress is to be applauded and reinforced. Things can only get better.

'Moving on is what we aim to do, and any form of progress is to be applauded and reinforced. Things can only get better'.

Summing Up

- The reinstatement of good mental health is essential if the individual is not to continue down the road that may well lead to successful suicide.

- The many factors that contribute to good mental health are available to everyone, however unlikely that may seem, and anyone who struggles with self-harm issues can find one or two small items amongst them. Then the job of returning to health and a full life can begin.

- Good mental health can always be approached, especially given patience and support. The goal to keep firmly in mind is 'to become the person you were meant to be'.

- Bad things happen in life, and we all respond to them. There is no shame in that. What is guaranteed is that as you begin to recover, you will emerge as bigger and stronger than you have ever been in your life, and the demons that haunt you will be vanquished forever.

Chapter Eleven

Scenarios and Exercises Discussed

Exercise 1. This preparation exercise asks you to examine your own reasons for wanting to understand more about self-harm. There are no right or wrong answers, since we all approach any study from an individual point of view. This is a good exercise to transfer to *any* study, before beginning to read the texts.

Exercise 2. By attempting this exercise in empathy, we can begin to imagine how the darkest times in life can overwhelm someone. There are bad times in every life, but for some the opportunity to talk and resolve the issues is not readily available. By completing this exercise, we can find out what we would like to be said, if we were struggling. Then when we are trying to help someone who self-harms, it is easier to remember what we might most usefully say.

Exercise 3. This exercise asks you to remember a situation in which you were bullied, and to consider how you would feel if you met that person now, years later. While the chance to tell them what you think of them may never present itself in real life, it is still good to imagine what you would say to them, to prove that they no longer can hurt you. We carry unresolved baggage around with us, from unresolved situations such as these. But it is still possible to deal with the emotions, many years on.

Exercise 4. Julie changes school, and leaves her friends and the situations she has known behind. The antagonism from a group of girls causes her massively increased anxiety, and begins to impact upon her body and her body image. This becomes a negative spiral, resulting in vomiting, headaches,

'We carry unresolved baggage around with us.'

weight loss and eventually cutting. The question 'what support is there to help Julie break free?' is crucial, but may still be hard to answer. If so, return to this later in the book, when further ideas may occur to you.

Exercise 5. In this exercise you are asked to consider meaningful occupation and what it might mean to you, then to consciously list the positives that arise from your choice. It is easy not to recognise how key this can be to self-image, and how strong a support it can be to good mental health, unless we do this consciously. Examine this concept and commit to making it part of life in the future.

Exercise 6. In this exercise you are asked to recall the good, positive things about your own childhood, and then to imagine one that is much worse. This will allow you to imagine what the certainties that a child from a bad situation carries forward into life, and to see how difficult it can be to break free of those perceptions and bad mental habits in later life.

Exercise 7. The two lists that you were asked to make in this exercise form the basis of the ways forward described in this book. Again, there are no right or wrong answers, since what works for each of us is a very individual thing.

Exercise 8. How we respond to others in times of need is crucial. It is easy to increase the damage to their self-esteem if we respond with anger and frustration. Questions are legitimate, but we should remember that they may not be answered, and that there is nothing personal in that. This may simply not be the right time. Quiet, gentle support – in the form of being with – is the best way forward. Health professionals should consider the words they might use, and practise these upon a colleague, who will then tell them how that question made them feel. We should always be ready to reflect and adapt in this way.

Exercise 9. Group work is the cornerstone of the support that can be offered to the self-harmer. The questions in this exercise may seem too simple or obvious to bother with, but in fact a group will fail if it is not clearly thought through, before it has begun. Those who come to group need to know that the facilitators understand what they are doing, are not 'experimenting' with them or may change the rules and boundaries halfway through. Inconsistency will damage trust and can be very destructive, wiping out all progress. The optimum number of group members is ten to twelve. This allows for a good range of backgrounds and personalities. Any more would be too difficult to manage and for members to feel ownership of. Too few may lead to one individual beginning to dominate the group, to the detriment of others. Given a good number, facilitators are not struggling as much with this, since a range of other members can be diverted to, if someone begins to dominate.

Exercise 10 (Scenario). This scenario deals with 'Carrie's' experience in accident and emergency. If you have experienced this scenario for yourself, or with someone you care about, you will know what a dreadful experience this can be. It also comes at a time when someone is at their most vulnerable. Health professionals will be aware that there is no time and space allocated to support or counselling in A and E, and it can easily appear that this is a dead-end situation with nothing to offer, except a deepening sense of shame. If, however, the right questions are asked, it is possible to take something away from the situation. A good department should be able to refer an individual to the mental health team, and this should be offered. If not, it can be asked for. Few departments do not have the Samaritans' number displayed on the wall, and if someone has found themselves in need of medical attention, they do need someone to talk to. The Samaritans will also be able to name local support groups. Finding oneself in A and E should be a wake-up call, to both patient and family. Now is the time for all concerned to admit there is a problem, and to set aside other issues, in order to resolve it.

Exercise 11. Ellen's situation is not as uncommon as you might think. Many people appear to succeed in life, but find an inner emptiness which seems never to be filled. The lesson from Ellen's scenario is that we are all creatures of many parts. Sometimes – and this is especially true of successful people – some of those parts are neglected. Eventually we forget what they were, but our minds and bodies still mourn their loss. Creativity, and all the joy that it can bring, are important parts of being human. If we allow ourselves to be creative, we can begin to establish ourselves as human beings again. The self-harmer's belief that they are 'less than human' is demolished by creative activities.

Help List

Al Anon

www.al-anonuk.org
Helpline: 020 7403 0888
For families and partners of anyone with a drink problem.
Site includes a guide to your nearest meeting.
Includes links to al-ateen.

Alateen

Alateen is for teenage relatives and friends of alcoholics. Alateen is part of Al-Anon. (see above)

Alcoholics Anonymous (AA)

Services are staffed by volunteer members of AA. For more general queries about AA you can write to the General Service Office:-

Alcoholics Anonymous,
PO Box 1,
10 Toft Green,
York YO1 7NJ
Helpline: 0845 769 7555
Email: help@alcoholics-anonymous.org.uk
www.alcoholics-anonymous.org.uk

Broken Rainbow

For LGBT victims of domestic abuse
www.broken-rainbow.org.uk
Helpline:0300 999 5428

Bully Free Zone

www.bullyfreezone.co.uk
Aims to 'raise awareness of alternative ways of resolving conflict and reducing bullying'.

'Now is the time for all concerned to admit there is a problem.'

Childline (c/o NSPCC)

Tel: 0800 1111
www.childline.org.uk

Drinkaware

www.drinkaware.co.uk
Outlines all you need to know about effects of alcohol, and when it is becoming a problem.

Gingerbread

www.gingerbread.org.uk
Provides advice and practical support for single parents.
Freephone: 0808 802 0925

MIND

www.mind.org.uk
Aims to help people take control of their mental health.
Infoline: 0300 123 3393 (also textphone at this number)
Email: info@mind.org.uk

Netmums

www.netmums.com
Excellent web-based forum where members offer support and ideas on every family problem under the sun.

NSPCC

www.nspcc.org.uk
Links to Childline (see above)
Tel: 0808 800 5000

Rape Crisis

www.rapecrisis.org.uk
Offers a series of support centres for women and girls across the country.
(Freephone) Tel: 0808 802 9999 (12-2.30pm and 7-9.30pm)

Refuge

www.refuge.org.uk
Tel: 0800 2000 247 (helpline) shared with Women's Aid.

Respect

www.respect.uk.net
For abusers who want to stop abusive behaviour.
Helpline: 0808 802 4040
Email: info@respect.uk.net

Samaritans

www.samaritans.org
24-hour source of support
UK helpline: 08457 90 90 90
Republic of Ireland helpline: 1850 60 90 90
Email: jo@samaritans.org
Write to: Chris, P.O. Box 9090, Stirling, FK8 2SA
(Can also operate face-to-face.)

Women's Aid

Women's Aid is the core service for women suffering from domestic violence.
They provide over 500 local services, including refuges, drop-in centres, a
quarterly magazine and a 24-hour free helpline.
Tel: 0800 2000 247 (helpline) shared with Refuge
Email: info@womensaid.org.uk
www.womensaid.org.uk
www.thehideout.org.uk (for children)

Zena

Committed to helping women fleeing from either culturally aggravated murder
(CAM) or domestic violence (DV).
info@zenafoundation.com

Glossary

Affect

Medical term for emotions. When affect is said to be flattened, the emotions are not registering normally. Individuals feel cut off from the world and from everyday feelings about it. They feel that their responses are not as they should be.

Body dysmorphic disorder (BDD)

A mental disorder characterised by distorted body image, and also by obsessions about perceived physical shortcomings.

Denial

A mental defense mechanism in which someone refuses to believe a fact that they cannot emotionally cope with. This may be despite overwhelming physical evidence. There are levels of denial, including a tendency to minimise the importance of an event. Denial is sometimes also referred to as abnegation.

Endorphins

Tiny protein molecules produced by the body. These are part of the body's natural challenge to pain and are produced in times of physical stress.

Holistic

Concerned with the 'whole' rather than component parts. Holistic care or therapy is based therefore upon the belief that mind, body, social factors and spirit are all interlinked, and that we are not effectively cared for if only one of these aspects is emphasised. This approach is now recognised as the best way of providing support, in any situation

Homeostasis

Steady state; the balanced parameters that the human body lives within, and the mechanisms to maintain that balance.

Paranoia

An excessive tendency to suspicion, and (very often) the belief that someone aims to harm us.

Projection
The tendency to attribute distressing emotions about oneself to someone else. (For instance, an unfaithful wife or husband may believe that their spouse is unfaithful.) Projection skews the individual's world view to a more acceptable set of scenarios.

PTSD (post-traumatic stress syndrome)
Caused by extreme stress, which may be physical, emotional or a combination of both. Several features, including hyperarousal and re-experiencing of the trauma (perhaps as flashbacks or nightmares). A numbing or flattening of affect and phobia may also develop.

Syndrome
A collection of signs and symptoms.

References

Caponecchia, Wyatt
Preventing Workplace Bullying
Routledge, 2011

Clark, M
Managing the Difficult Child
Northcote House, 1999

Ginott et al
Between Parent and Child
Three Rivers Press, New York, 2004

Grant, Biley, Walker (editors)
Our Encounters with Madness
PCCS Books, 2011

Klonsky, ED
The Functions of Deliberate Self-injury; A Review of the Evidence
Clinical Psychology Review 27 (2) 226-239, 2007

Maslow, Abraham (1954)
Motivation and Personality. New York: Harper. pp. 236

Muehlenkamp, J. J. (2005)
Self-Injurious Behavior as a Separate Clinical Syndrome,
 American Journal of Orthopsychiatry 75 (2): 324–333,

Skegg, K. (2005)
Self-harm, Lancet 336: 1471

Thomson J,
Bullying; A Parent's Guide
Need2Know, 2010

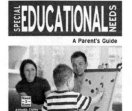

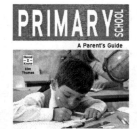

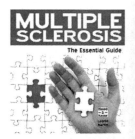